Lesson 1
The Robber Bees

● Read the story below. The new words for you to learn are in dark print. Think of what these words could mean as you read.

The Robber Bees

The **robber** bees make their living by taking things that do not belong to them. They do not even make their own nests. They take them away from other bees. They rob others for their food, too. It is **possible** for these bees to **force** other bees into doing what they want. Yet, these robber bees have no **stinger.** They use a kind of insect spray to get their way.

Here is how the thieves work. One or two of the thieves **enter** into the nest they want to rob. There they give off a spray that smells like lemons. Without a **battle** the other bees leave their honey behind and rush away to the room where the baby bees are kept. A large number of thieves then **crowd** into the nest. They take wax and honey which they **carry** to their own nest. The hold-up lasts **several** hours or even a day or two. After a time, the **greedy** thieves leave and let the honey bees be.

Getting the Details

● Circle the number of the word which best answers the following question:

Which of these is *not* needed by the robber bees?

1) wax

2) honey

3) a stinger

4) a spray

Working with the Alphabet

● Write the following vocabulary words from the story in alphabetical order on the lines below.

robber	several	stinger	carry	crowd
enter	force	battle	possible	greedy

1. _____ 6. _____

2. _____ 7. _____

3. _____ 8. _____

4. _____ 9. _____

5. _____ 10. _____

Matching Words with Meanings

▲ Context clues are words in a sentence that give you a clue to the meaning of a vocabulary word.

● Reread the story. Look for context clues for each vocabulary word as you read. Then match each vocabulary word with its meaning. Write the letter of the meaning on the line next to the word. If you need help, find the meanings of the words in the glossary at the back of this book.

_____ 1. greedy

_____ 2. force

_____ 3. battle

_____ 4. enter

_____ 5. robber

_____ 6. crowd

_____ 7. several

_____ 8. possible

_____ 9. carry

_____ 10. stinger

a. a person who steals by using force or threats

b. the part of an insect used to hurt by pricking

c. more than two but not many; a few

d. wanting or taking all that one can get with no thought of what others need; selfish

e. to come or go in or into

f. that can be

g. to take from one place to another; transport or conduct

h. any fight or struggle; conflict

i. to come together in a large group

j. to make do something by using strength or power of some kind

4

Completing the Sentences

● Read the sentences below. Write the vocabulary words that best complete the sentences.

stinger	greedy	enter	battle	robber
carry	crowd	possible	forced	Several

1. Is it _____ for a bee to live without its _____?

2. One _____ was too _____ because he was caught when he came back for more.

3. When Jane broke her foot on the hike, her dad was _____ to _____ her on his back.

4. If it rains, the children will _____ the door and _____ together in the small hall.

5. _____ dogs were in a _____ over a small piece of meat.

Working with Antonyms

▲ **Antonyms** are words that have opposite meanings. For example, *large* and *small*, *cold* and *hot* are antonyms.

● Use the word list to find an antonym for each puzzle word shown. Then write the antonyms in the boxes.

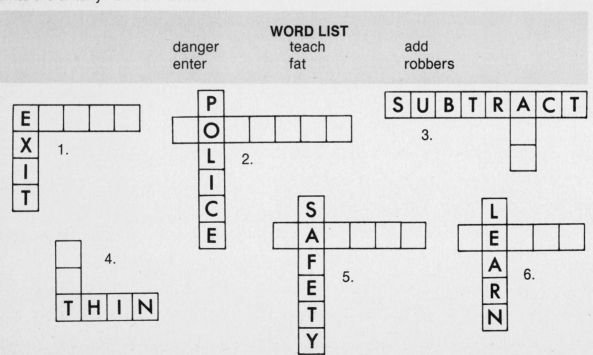

WORD LIST

danger	teach	add
enter	fat	robbers

Taking a Test

● Read each phrase. Fill in the oval next to the best meaning for the word in dark print.

1. **carry** the heavy load
   - Ⓐ unload
   - Ⓑ find
   - Ⓒ transport

2. a **greedy** giant
   - Ⓐ large
   - Ⓑ selfish
   - Ⓒ quick-moving

3. **possible** showers
   - Ⓐ likely
   - Ⓑ heavy
   - Ⓒ light

4. for **several** days
   - Ⓐ short
   - Ⓑ not the same
   - Ⓒ a few

5. **crowd** into a circle
   - Ⓐ come together
   - Ⓑ make a ring
   - Ⓒ ran after another

6. **battle** over the land
   - Ⓐ fight
   - Ⓑ plow
   - Ⓒ hurry

7. **force** them to go
   - Ⓐ use strength to make
   - Ⓑ ask
   - Ⓒ wish

8. **enter** the store
   - Ⓐ work in
   - Ⓑ clean up
   - Ⓒ go into

9. used its **stinger**
   - Ⓐ part that pricks
   - Ⓑ person that sings
   - Ⓒ thing that smells bad

10. saw the **robber**
    - Ⓐ kind of shoe
    - Ⓑ person who steals
    - Ⓒ band for papers

Challenging Yourself: Scrambled Words

● The letters in each of your vocabulary words have been scrambled. Use the word list to help you spell each word correctly. Write the words on the lines.

1. g r e n i s t _____

2. d e r e g y _____

3. w r o d c _____

4. r e n t e _____

5. s a l r e v e _____

6. b o r r e b _____

7. r o c f e _____

8. t a t b e l _____

9. b o s l e s p i _____

10. y r a c r _____

WORD LIST
force
carry
enter
stinger
robber
several
greedy
crowd
battle
possible

Using Words You Know: Narrative Writing

● Look at the picture below. Write a story about what happened. The following questions will guide you in your writing. What if you were coming home from school and found someone taking something from your friend's house? What would you do? What would happen to the robber? How would you feel after this adventure?

　　Use at least three words from the vocabulary lesson in your story.

_____

_____

_____

_____

_____

_____

_____

_____

_____

_____

_____

_____

Lesson 2
Tailorbird

● Read the story below. The new words for you to learn are in dark print. Think of what these words could mean as you read.

Tailorbird

A **tailor** is a person who **sews** for a living. In a land far away, there is a bird that sews for its family. It is called a tailorbird. The **male** bird **prepares** a nest for the **female** to lay her eggs. He finds two big leaves hanging close together on a tree and makes a nest of them. Here is how he does it.

The little bird **pokes** holes in the leaves with his bill. Then he finds thread from a spider web or a plant. He **knots** the thread and puts it in and out of the holes, stitching the two leaves together around the bottom. Next, he finds **material** to make the nest **fluffy** inside. At last the nest is ready for the female. She will put her eggs in the tiny little nest. Her babies will soon be **hatched.**

Getting the Details

● Circle the number of the word or words which best answers the following question:

What does the tailorbird use to make holes in the leaves?

1) thread

2) his bill

3) fluffy material

4) a hatchet

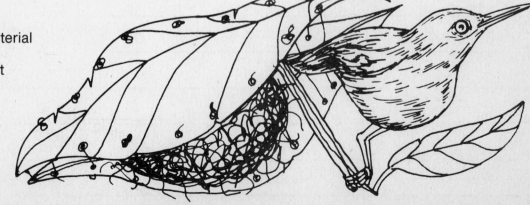

Working with the Alphabet

● Write the following vocabulary words from the story in alphabetical order on the lines below.

tailor   sews   male   female   pokes

prepares   material   fluffy   hatched   knots

1. _____   6. _____

2. _____   7. _____

3. _____   8. _____

4. _____   9. _____

5. _____   10. _____

Matching Words with Meanings

● Reread the story. Use context clues or the glossary to match each vocabulary word below with its meaning. Write the letter of the meaning on the line next to the word.

_____ 1. fluffy

_____ 2. poke

_____ 3. male

_____ 4. hatch

_____ 5. material

_____ 6. knot

_____ 7. prepare

_____ 8. sew

_____ 9. tailor

_____ 10. female

a. of or for women or girls

b. to make or get ready

c. soft and light like fluff

d. to fasten with stitches made with needle and thread

e. cloth or other fabric

f. to bring forth young birds, fish, turtles, etc. from eggs

g. a fastening made by tying together parts or pieces of string, rope, etc.

h. a person who makes or repairs suits, coats, etc.

i. of or for men or boys

j. to push or jab, as with a stick, finger, etc.

Completing the Sentences

● Read the sentences below. Write the vocabulary words that best complete the sentences.

tailor	sew	male	female	poked
preparing	material	fluffy	hatch	knots

1. My mother knows how to _____ clothes.

2. She bought some flowered _____ to make a new dress.

3. The _____ put new buttons on the suit.

4. He tied _____ in the thread so they would stay in place.

5. Sally _____ her finger through a small hole in her pillow.

6. Inside she could feel the _____ feathers.

7. Mary is _____ a home for some chicks.

8. The eggs will _____ very soon.

9. Most _____ birds are brightly colored so they will attract a mate.

10. The _____ birds have dull colors so they can hide in the nest.

Working with Homonyms

▲ **Homonyms** are words that sound alike but have different meanings and spellings. For example, *know* and *no* are homonyms.

● Draw lines to match the homonyms below.

1. creak	a. hair		4. break	a. heal
2. or	b. oar		5. die	b. brake
3. hare	c. creek		6. heel	c. dye

● Use the homonyms from above to complete the sentences below.

a. We could have soup _____ a sandwich for lunch.

b. There is a small bridge over the _____ .

c. You should comb your _____ for the picture.

d. The _____ of Mary's shoe is worn down.

e. Many house plants _____ in the winter.

f. Did you _____ that window with that ball?

Taking a Test

● Read each phrase. Fill in the oval next to the best meaning for the word in dark print.

1. watched the **tailor**
   - Ⓐ person who repairs suits
   - Ⓑ person who makes bread
   - Ⓒ person who watches birds

2. a **male** animal
   - Ⓐ large
   - Ⓑ wild
   - Ⓒ boy

3. learned to **sew**
   - Ⓐ read
   - Ⓑ stitch
   - Ⓒ bake

4. **poked** a hole in
   - Ⓐ scratched
   - Ⓑ jabbed
   - Ⓒ rubbed

5. a **fluffy** cloud
   - Ⓐ dark
   - Ⓑ rain
   - Ⓒ soft

6. **hatched** the eggs
   - Ⓐ boiled
   - Ⓑ brought forth young
   - Ⓒ ate

7. tied a **knot**
   - Ⓐ bow
   - Ⓑ ribbon
   - Ⓒ fastening

8. bought some **material**
   - Ⓐ cloth
   - Ⓑ paper
   - Ⓒ thread

9. a **female** insect
   - Ⓐ scary
   - Ⓑ girl
   - Ⓒ common

10. **prepared** for school
    - Ⓐ made ready
    - Ⓑ left
    - Ⓒ walked

Challenging Yourself: Word Search

● The ten vocabulary words from this lesson appear in the word search below. Some are written across, while others are written up and down. Find each word in the word search and circle it. The vocabulary words are listed in the box to help you.

```
I N Y W E K B T M L
T A M O R N F L A U
F T A I L O R F T Y
H R L E A T D P E P
O F E M A L E O R K
E F M S R E P K I A
S P R E P A R E A T
E W S W C B L A L I
O R F L U F F Y O T
S O H A T C H R F Y
```

WORD LIST

sew

male

female

knot

material

prepare

tailor

poke

hatch

fluffy

Using Words You Know: Descriptive Writing

● Look at the picture below. Write three sentences telling about the robin. The following questions will help guide you in writing your sentences. What body parts does a robin have? What color is the bird? How large is the robin?

    Use at least three words from this vocabulary lesson in your sentences.

_____

_____

_____

_____

_____

_____

_____

_____

_____

_____

_____

Lesson 3
An Amazing Plant

● Read the story below. The new words for you to learn are in dark print. Think of what these words could mean as you read.

An Amazing Plant

The resurrection (rez′ ə rek′ shen) plant is really a very **amazing** plant. It can dry up, blow away, and then come back to life. Its name even means "to come back from the dead." This plant is also one of the few that can **wander** from place to place.

The resurrection plant lives in the **desert.** Since it hardly ever rains there, water is very **scarce.** When there is too little **moisture,** the plant dries up. Its roots come out of the ground. The whole plant is a ball of **twigs** that looks dead. As it **drifts,** it can **search** for water. When it finds enough moisture, the **roots** sink back into the ground. What seemed to be a dead plant returns to life. The leaves **sprout** and the plant grows again. When the desert again becomes dry, the plant will pull up its roots and leave. Once again it will wander across the desert to look for water. Then, it can come back to life and bloom again.

Getting the Details

● Circle the number of the sentence which best answers the following question:

What happens to the plant when it comes to water?

1) Its roots come out of the ground.

2) It wanders around the desert.

3) It dies and becomes dried twigs.

4) Its roots grow into the ground.

Working with the Alphabet

● Write the following vocabulary words from the story in alphabetical order on the lines below.

search	desert	drifts	scarce	sprout
amazing	roots	twigs	wander	moisture

1. _____   6. _____

2. _____   7. _____

3. _____   8. _____

4. _____   9. _____

5. _____   10. _____

Matching Words with Meanings

● Reread the story. Use context clues or the glossary to match each vocabulary word below with its meaning. Write the letter of the meaning on the line next to the word.

_____ 1. desert

_____ 2. amazing

_____ 3. root

_____ 4. sprout

_____ 5. scarce

_____ 6. drift

_____ 7. moisture

_____ 8. wander

_____ 9. search

_____ 10. twig

a. to go from place to place in an aimless way; ramble; roam

b. the part of a plant that grows in the ground, where it holds the plant in place and takes water and food from the soil

c. to try to find

d. not common; rarely seen

e. to be carried along by a current of water or air

f. to begin to grow

g. liquid causing a dampness, as fine drops of water in the air

h. a small branch or shoot of a tree or shrub

i. a dry sandy region with little or no plant life

j. causing great surprise or wonder

Completing the Sentences

● Read the sentences below. Write the vocabulary words that best complete the sentences.

moisture   roots   amazing   wandered   search
drifted   sprout   twigs   desert   scarce

1. The strong wind blew some _____ off the tree.

2. The little lost child _____ around the park.

3. Carrots and potatoes are really the _____ of those plants.

4. We watched the magician perform _____ tricks with a rope.

5. The snow _____ over the roads and sidewalks.

6. In the spring tulips will _____ .

7. The short rain brought a little _____ to the dry grass.

8. Ned will _____ for his missing notebook.

9. Water is _____ in the desert.

10. The cactus is a plant that lives in the _____.

Working with Endings

▲ **Endings** can be added to many words. Sometimes the spelling of a word must be changed when an ending is added.

● Read the rules for adding endings below. Then do the exercise below.

Rule 1: Add **s** to make most words plural.   *book, books*
Rule 2: Add **es** if a word ends in ch, sh, s, or x.   *punch, punches, punched, punching*
Rule 3: If a word ends in consonant-y, change the **y** to **i** and add the ending **es** or **ed**.   *copy, copies, copied, copying*
Rule 4: If a short-vowel word ends in a single consonant, double the final consonant before adding **ed** or **ing**.   *drop, drops, dropped, dropping*
Rule 5: If a word ends in an e, drop the e before adding **ed** or **ing**.   *wipe, wipes, wiped, wiping*

● Add the endings **s** or **es, ed,** and **ing** to the words listed. Check the ending rules to see if spelling changes are needed.

WORD	S or ES	ED	ING
1. search	_____	_____	_____
2. carry	_____	_____	_____
3. hope	_____	_____	_____
4. drip	_____	_____	_____

Taking a Test

● Read each phrase. Fill in the oval next to the best meaning for the word in dark print.

1. **drifts** over the prairie
   - Ⓐ rides
   - Ⓑ is carried by the wind
   - Ⓒ is carried on horseback

2. a long **search**
   - Ⓐ hunt
   - Ⓑ tiring day
   - Ⓒ hard problem

3. broken **twigs**
   - Ⓐ toys
   - Ⓑ branches
   - Ⓒ promises

4. pulled the **roots**
   - Ⓐ weeds
   - Ⓑ plant part
   - Ⓒ wagons

5. **sprout** up overnight
   - Ⓐ plant
   - Ⓑ begin to grow
   - Ⓒ fly

6. an **amazing** animal
   - Ⓐ causing wonder
   - Ⓑ smart
   - Ⓒ fast

7. **wander** through the park
   - Ⓐ drive
   - Ⓑ roam
   - Ⓒ jog

8. a **desert** home
   - Ⓐ land with many plants
   - Ⓑ large neighborhood
   - Ⓒ dry sandy area

9. a **scarce** jewel
   - Ⓐ beautiful
   - Ⓑ uncommon
   - Ⓒ dull

10. felt the **moisture**
    - Ⓐ cloth
    - Ⓑ softness
    - Ⓒ wetness

Challenging Yourself: Analogies

▲ **Analogies** show us the relationships between things. For example, *book* is to *read* as *song* is to *sing*. *Finger* is to *hand* as *toe* is to *foot*.
● Complete the following analogies using the words listed in the box below.

1. **sand** is to _____ as **ice** is to **glacier**

2. _____ is to **plentiful** as **few** is to **many**

3. **bird** is to **nest** as _____ is to **den**

4. _____ is to **dirt** as **branches** is to **air**

5. **electricity** is to **lightning** as _____ is to **cloud**

6. _____ is to **discover** as **seek** is to **find**

WORD LIST
moisture
scarce
lion
search
roots
desert

16

Using Words You Know: Comparative Writing

● Look at the pictures below. Write three sentences comparing the tree and the bush. The following questions will help guide you in writing your sentences. What do you see growing on each plant? What do both plants need in order to grow? What is different about the plants?

Use at least three words from this vocabulary lesson in your sentences.

_____

_____

_____

_____

_____

_____

_____

_____

_____

_____

_____

_____

Lesson 4
The Kangaroo's Tail

● Read the story below. The new words for you to learn are in dark print. Think of what these words could mean as you read.

The Kangaroo's Tail

People know **kangaroos** carry their babies in a **pouch.** They do not know kangaroos carry a chair and a **crutch,** too. The chair and the crutch are really their tails.

The kangaroo's tail is very **powerful.** A kangaroo never has to look for a seat. It just sits down. Its strong tail becomes a chair.

Its tail helps it **travel** from place to place. To walk, the kangaroo puts down its front paws. It puts its tail under its heavy body. It uses its tail like a crutch. The tail holds up the whole back part of the body as the back legs swing along **forward.**

To go fast a kangaroo jumps. It could **leap** across a classroom or over an **automobile** in one jump. It can go fast. It uses its tail to keep its **balance** as it speeds along.

Next time you want to tell a story, why not tell the strange **tale** of the kangaroo's tail?

Getting the Details

● Circle the number of the words which best answers the following question:

What is one thing a kangaroo can jump over?

1)   a school building

2)   a mountain

3)   a car

4)   a circus tent

18

Working with the Alphabet

● Write the following vocabulary words from the story in alphabetical order on the lines below.

leap	balance	pouch	kangaroos	automobile
crutch	powerful	travel	forward	tale

1. _____
2. _____
3. _____
4. _____
5. _____

6. _____
7. _____
8. _____
9. _____
10. _____

Matching Words with Meanings

● Reread the story. Use context clues or the glossary to match each vocabulary word below with its meaning. Write the letter of the meaning on the line next to the word.

_____ 1. kangaroo

_____ 2. pouch

_____ 3. crutch

_____ 4. powerful

_____ 5. forward

_____ 6. leap

_____ 7. balance

_____ 8. tale

_____ 9. automobile

_____ 10. travel

a. a kind of support

b. to the front; ahead

c. a story, especially about things that are imagined or made up

d. an animal of Australia with short forelegs and strong, large hind legs, with which it makes long leaps

e. a car; motorcar

f. to move oneself suddenly from the ground by using the leg muscles; jump; spring

g. to go from one place to another

h. having much power; strong or influential

i. a loose fold of skin, like a pocket, on the belly of certain female animals, as the kangaroo, in which they carry their newborn young

j. the ability to keep one's body steady without falling; stability

19

Completing the Sentences

● Read the sentences below. Write the vocabulary words that best complete the sentences.

kangaroo	forward	tale	pouch	powerful
traveled	leaped	balance	automobile	crutches

1. The tow truck pulled the _____ from the ditch.

2. Its _____ engine roared as it pulled the heavy weight.

3. Jane wrote a _____ about a talking mouse from Mars.

4. The mouse _____ to earth by rocket.

5. I like to watch the _____ when I visit the zoo.

6. Sometimes I can see a baby kangaroo peeking out of its mother's _____.

7. Rich has had to use _____ since he broke his leg.

8. He is looking _____ to having the cast removed from his leg.

9. Jenny kept her _____ beautifully while walking on the beam.

10. Then she _____ off it and landed just right on the mat.

Working with Suffixes

▲ A **root word** is a word or word part that is used as a base for making other words. Other parts can be added to the beginning or end of a root word.

A **suffix** is a word part that can be added to the end of a root word. Adding a suffix changes the meaning of the root word.

The suffix **ful** means *full of* or *likely to.*

● Look at the sentences below. Complete the sentences by adding the suffix **ful** to the root word that is underlined.

1. If a machine is full of power, it is _____.

2. If you are full of joy, you are _____.

3. If you are full of thought, you are _____.

4. If a picture is full of color, it is _____.

5. If you are likely to forget, you are _____.

6. If you are full of care, you are _____.

7. If you are likely to help, you are _____.

8. If you are full of cheer, you are _____.

20

Taking a Test

● Read each phrase. Fill in the oval next to the best meaning for the word in dark print.

1. watched a **kangaroo**
   - Ⓐ person at the zoo
   - Ⓑ baby in a cradle
   - Ⓒ animal with a pouch

2. stepped **forward**
   - Ⓐ back
   - Ⓑ ahead
   - Ⓒ over

3. used a **crutch**
   - Ⓐ a support
   - Ⓑ pole
   - Ⓒ pencil

4. heard a **tale**
   - Ⓐ song
   - Ⓑ sound
   - Ⓒ story

5. a **powerful** arm
   - Ⓐ weak
   - Ⓑ strong
   - Ⓒ broken

6. will **leap** across
   - Ⓐ jump
   - Ⓑ swim
   - Ⓒ walk

7. bought an **automobile**
   - Ⓐ truck
   - Ⓑ plane
   - Ⓒ car

8. lost his **balance**
   - Ⓐ lunch money
   - Ⓑ stability
   - Ⓒ way home

9. **travel** to another city
   - Ⓐ go
   - Ⓑ come
   - Ⓒ run

10. in the kangaroo's **pouch**
    - Ⓐ center of the room
    - Ⓑ animal's cage
    - Ⓒ fold of skin

Challenging Yourself: Picture Identification

● Look at the pictures below. Write the vocabulary word from the word list that is suggested by each picture.

WORD LIST			
tale	leap	balance	pouch
kangaroo	travel	crutch	automobile

1.

2.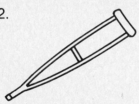

3.

4.

5.

6.

7.

8.

Using Words You Know: Persuasive Writing

● Look at the pictures below. Write three sentences trying to talk your parents into taking you to the zoo to see the kangaroos. The following questions will help guide you in writing your sentences. Why do you want to see the kangaroos? How have you been behaving in the past week? What have you learned about kangaroos in school?

   Use at least three words from this vocabulary lesson in your sentences.

_____

_____

_____

_____

_____

_____

_____

_____

_____

_____

Lesson 5
The Real Life of Tom Thumb

● Read the story below. The new words for you to learn are in dark print. Think of what these words could mean as you read.

The Real Life of Tom Thumb

When the man **known** as Tom Thumb was full-grown, he was only a little bigger than a two-year-old child. How could a **real person** be so small? People could not believe it!

When Tom Thumb was four, people began to hear of him. They paid money to see him sing and dance. Kings and queens wanted to see him **perform.** As he traveled with his show, he took a ladder along so he could climb into bed. He rode through streets in a tiny **carriage.** It was pulled by tiny ponies.

By the time he was eight, he was **rich.** When he was older, he owned a boat and lived in a **mansion.**

At twenty-five Tom fell in love with a beautiful young lady. She, like Tom, was a **midget.** At their **wedding,** the **couple** looked like little dolls. Their wedding cake weighed more than Tom and his wife combined!

Tom and his wife traveled all over the world. Tom Thumb lived about one hundred years ago. At that time he was one of the best-known men on earth.

Getting the Details

● Circle the number of the phrase which best answers the following question:

How long ago did Tom Thumb live?

1) about twenty-five years ago

2) more than four hundred years ago

3) about one hundred years ago

4) less than twenty-five years ago

Working with the Alphabet

● Write the following vocabulary words from the story in alphabetical order on the lines below.

midget   known   person   carriage   rich

perform   mansion   couple   real   wedding

1. _____   6. _____

2. _____   7. _____

3. _____   8. _____

4. _____   9. _____

5. _____   10. _____

Matching Words with Meanings

● Reread the story. Use context clues or the glossary to match each vocabulary word below with its meaning. Write the letter of the meaning on the line next to the word.

_____ 1. person

_____ 2. perform

_____ 3. carriage

_____ 4. rich

_____ 5. mansion

_____ 6. midget

_____ 7. wedding

_____ 8. couple

_____ 9. known

_____ 10. real

a. having wealth; owning much money or property; wealthy

b. marriage or the marriage ceremony

c. to do something to entertain an audience; act, play music, sing, etc.

d. a man and woman who are married, engaged, or partners, as in a dance

e. a large, stately house

f. a human being; man, woman, or child

g. a vehicle with wheels, usually one drawn by horses, for carrying people

h. being such or happening so in fact; not imagined; true; actual

i. recognized; noted

j. a very small person

Completing the Sentences

● Read the sentences below. Write the vocabulary words that best complete the sentences.

couple	mansion	performing	rich	wedding
carriage	midget	known	real	person

1. Princess Diana arrived for her _____ in a horse-drawn

    _____.

2. The _____ family lived in a beautiful, large

    _____.

3. The _____ Tom Thumb was _____

    throughout the world.

4. The robot looked like a _____ _____.

5. The _____ had been _____ together in the

    circus for many years.

Working with Prefixes

▲ A **prefix** is a word part that can be added to the beginning of a root word. Adding a prefix changes the meaning of the root word.
        The prefix **un** means *not* or *opposite of.*

● Read each meaning below. Add the prefix **un** to each underlined word. Write the new word on the line.

MEANING	NEW WORD
1. not <u>real</u>	_____
2. opposite of <u>tie</u>	_____
3. opposite of <u>wrap</u>	_____
4. not <u>eaten</u>	_____

● Use the new words above to complete the sentences below.

a. Please _____ my shoelace.

b. Jim left the table with his supper _____

c. You should know that ghosts are _____.

d. Janet will _____ her presents on her birthday.

Taking a Test

● Read each phrase. Fill in the oval next to the best meaning for the word in dark print.

1. a **rich** brother
   - Ⓐ sick
   - Ⓑ wealthy
   - Ⓒ kind

2. saw her **perform**
   - Ⓐ entertain
   - Ⓑ leave
   - Ⓒ again

3. an old **person**
   - Ⓐ book
   - Ⓑ story
   - Ⓒ human

4. in the **carriage**
   - Ⓐ building
   - Ⓑ vehicle
   - Ⓒ horse

5. a summer **wedding**
   - Ⓐ trip
   - Ⓑ storm
   - Ⓒ marriage

6. a brick **mansion**
   - Ⓐ house
   - Ⓑ fence
   - Ⓒ street

7. **known** by that name
   - Ⓐ called
   - Ⓑ baptized
   - Ⓒ recognized

8. a friendly **couple**
   - Ⓐ pair
   - Ⓑ pet
   - Ⓒ answer

9. the **real** time
   - Ⓐ first
   - Ⓑ only
   - Ⓒ true

10. the **midget** worked
    - Ⓐ tall person
    - Ⓑ sad clown
    - Ⓒ small person

Challenging Yourself: Crossword Puzzle

● Read the clues below. Use the vocabulary words from the box to complete the crossword puzzle.

WORD LIST
person
real
known
carriage
wedding
rich
couple
midget
perform
mansion

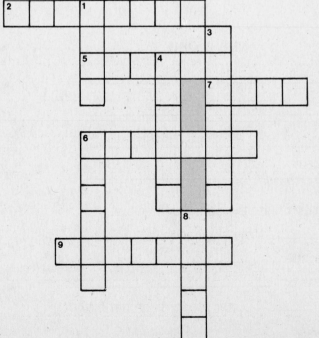

ACROSS
2. horse-drawn vehicle
5. a man and a woman
6. large house
7. true, actual
9. marriage of a man and a woman

DOWN
1. having much money
3. to entertain
4. a human being
6. a small person
8. recognized

Using Words You Know: Creative Writing

● Pretend that you wake up one morning to find you shrank in height. Every day you get shorter and shorter. Write a story telling about your experience. Then draw a picture of yourself in the box below. The following questions will help guide you in writing your story. What do you look like now? How do you feel? How do you do things differently now? How small are you?

Use at least three vocabulary words from this lesson in your sentences.

Lesson 6
Dreams

● Read the story below. The new words for you to learn are in dark print. Think of what these words could mean as you read.

Dreams

Dreams are like stories people watch in their sleep. People have **studied** dreams. Here is what they have found. Everyone dreams. Most **adults** dream from three to five times in one night. Each dream lasts from ten to thirty minutes. People dream about things that have just happened. They dream about events they have thought about **recently.** They **hardly** ever dream about things that took place more than two days before.

Most people dream in color. People who have always been **blind,** however, do not see anything **during** their dreams. They dream of sounds, feelings, tastes, and smells.

People do not dream when they are in deep or **sound** sleep. They dream during times when they are nearly awake. Dreaming is helpful **though.** People who were not **allowed** to dream became very **grouchy.** People often say grouchy people "got up on the wrong side of the bed." Maybe they should say, "Go back and dream awhile!"

Getting the Main Idea

● Circle the number of the phrase which best answers the following question:

What is the best main idea of this story?

1) things people find out when they studied dreams

2) most people dream in color

3) dreams that have come true

4) an old saying about getting out of bed

Working with the Alphabet

● Write the following vocabulary words from the story in alphabetical order on the lines below.

recently   blind   grouchy   sound   adults

allowed   though   studied   hardly   during

1. _____   6. _____

2. _____   7. _____

3. _____   8. _____

4. _____   9. _____

5. _____   10. _____

Matching Words with Meanings

● Reread the story. Use context clues or the glossary to match each vocabulary word below with its meaning. Write the letter of the meaning on the line next to the word.

_____ 1. study

_____ 2. adult

_____ 3. recently

_____ 4. hardly

_____ 5. blind

_____ 6. during

_____ 7. though

_____ 8. allow

_____ 9. grouchy

_____ 10. sound

a. only just; almost not; scarcely

b. to let be done; permit; let

c. deep and undisturbed

d. to look at or into carefully; examine or investigate

e. throughout the whole time of; all through

f. a man or woman who is fully grown up; mature person

g. to be in a bad or grumbling mood; cross and complaining

h. not able to see; having no sight

i. of a time just before now; lately

j. in spite of the fact that; although; however

Completing the Sentences

● Read the sentences below. Write the vocabulary words that best complete the sentences.

blind	grouchy	sound	allowed	adults
hardly	during	though	recently	study

1. Ben tried to _____ on the playground.

2. It was too noisy, _____.

3. The _____ ate at a large table in the dining room.

4. All the children were _____ to eat outside at the picnic table.

5. Mr. Swanson has been _____ for a long time.

6. He can tell where people are by how far away they _____.

7. Mrs. Jackson _____ ever smiles.

8. She is always _____ no matter what happens!

9. My sister _____ won first place in a gymnastics contest.

10. I held my breath _____ her whole performance.

Working with Suffixes

▲ A **suffix** is a word part that can be added to the end of a root word.
Adding a suffix changes the meaning of the word.
        The suffix **ly** means *in a way*.

● Read each meaning below. Add the suffix **ly** to each underlined word.
Write the new word on the line.

MEANING	NEW WORD
1. in a <u>recent</u> time	_____
2. in a <u>slow</u> way	_____
3. in a <u>sad</u> way	_____
4. in a <u>quick</u> way	_____

● Use the new words from above to complete the sentences below.

a. _____, the two friends went off to separate schools.

b. _____, we moved into our new house.

c. Turtles crawl very _____.

d. The runners raced very _____.

Taking a Test

● Read each phrase. Fill in the oval next to the best meaning for the word in dark print.

1. listen to **adults**
   - Ⓐ grown-ups
   - Ⓑ children
   - Ⓒ records

2. was late, **though**
   - Ⓐ maybe
   - Ⓑ however
   - Ⓒ also

3. is not **allowed**
   - Ⓐ here
   - Ⓑ time
   - Ⓒ permitted

4. heard it **recently**
   - Ⓐ clearly
   - Ⓑ not on purpose
   - Ⓒ a short time ago

5. a **blind** dog
   - Ⓐ big
   - Ⓑ sightless
   - Ⓒ mean

6. had a **sound** sleep
   - Ⓐ deep
   - Ⓑ restless
   - Ⓒ noisy

7. **studied** the problem
   - Ⓐ caused
   - Ⓑ asked a question
   - Ⓒ looked at closely

8. **during** the storm
   - Ⓐ before
   - Ⓑ all through
   - Ⓒ after

9. a **grouchy** mood
   - Ⓐ cross
   - Ⓑ good
   - Ⓒ tired

10. **hardly** had time
    - Ⓐ usually
    - Ⓑ never
    - Ⓒ scarcely

Challenging Yourself: Riddle

● To find the answer to the riddle, write the words on the blanks next to their clues. The answer will appear in the shaded column. Use the word list to help you.

Riddle: This dream is frightening and may cause you to wake up.

CLUES

1. a noise

2. no sight

3. in a bad mood

4. however

5. look at carefully

6. do while sleeping

7. grown-up

8. all through

9. a short time ago

WORD LIST

sound

though

study

adult

grouchy

during

recently

blind

dream

Using Words You Know: Narrative Writing

● Look at the picture below. The child in the picture is dreaming. Write a short paragraph about a dream you have had. The following questions will help guide you in writing your paragraph. Who was in your dream? What happened? How did your dream make you feel?

Use at least three words from this vocabulary lesson in your paragraph.

_____

_____

_____

_____

_____

_____

_____

_____

_____

_____

_____

Lesson 7
"Little House" Lady

● Read the story below. The new words for you to learn are in dark print. Think of what these words could mean as you read.

"Little House" Lady

The **television** show "Little House on the Prairie" has made-up stories about some people who really lived. Laura Ingalls was a real girl. She was **born** about one hundred fifty years ago in a little log **cabin** in the big north woods. She went West with her Ma and Pa and her sister Mary in a covered wagon. They moved to Kansas and lived in a "little house on the **prairie.**" They moved to new **territories** that had just opened up to **settlers.** When Laura was a grown woman, she wrote many books about her family's adventures. Her books are very **interesting.** They are like time machines. They take our **minds** through time and **space** into the **past.** We can see just how people lived long ago.

In all, Laura Ingalls Wilder wrote ten books. In time to come, you may want to read them all.

Getting the Main Idea

● Circle the number of the phrase which best answers the following question:

What is this story mainly about?

1) a little house on a prairie

2) a covered wagon that went to Kansas

3) a time machine

4) a lady who wrote about her life long ago

Working with the Alphabet

● Write the following vocabulary words from the story in alphabetical order on the lines below.

cabin   interesting   past   minds   television

prairie   settlers   space   born   territories

1. _____   6. _____

2. _____   7. _____

3. _____   8. _____

4. _____   9. _____

5. _____   10. _____

Matching Words with Meanings

● Reread the story. Use context clues or the glossary to match each vocabulary word below with its meaning. Write the letter of the meaning on the line next to the word.

_____ 1. television

_____ 2. born

_____ 3. cabin

_____ 4. prairie

_____ 5. territory

_____ 6. settler

_____ 7. interesting

_____ 8. mind

_____ 9. space

_____ 10. past

a. any large stretch of land; region

b. stirring up one's interest; exciting attention

c. brought into life or being

d. of, using, used in, or sent by television

e. the area that stretches in all directions, has no limits, and contains all things in the universe

f. the part of a person that thinks, reasons, feels, decides, etc.; intellect

g. gone by; ended; over

h. a person or thing that settles in a new country

i. a small house built in a simple, rough way, usually of wood

j. a large area of level or rolling grassy land without many trees

Completing the Sentences

● Read the paragraph below. Write the vocabulary words that best complete the sentences.

prairie	minds	television	cabins	interesting
past	space	born	territory	settlers

We can learn much by studying our country's _____. Early

_____ had much unexplored land from which to choose a place to live.

They built very small sod _____ on the plains. It could be a lonely life

because they had few close neighbors on the broad, treeless, grassy _____.

Families had plenty of _____ to do their farming, though.

There was no _____ for entertainment. Boys and girls stretched

their _____ by reading, talking, and playing games. As soon as

a _____ became settled, it would soon become a state.

This _____ way of life will never return. In fact, it was all over before

any of us were _____.

Working with Syllables

● Words can be divided into smaller word parts, or **syllables.** Say each word and listen for the syllables. Write each word below leaving a space between syllables. Use a dictionary if you are not sure where to divide a word.

1. television   _____
2. prairie   _____
3. territory   _____
4. adventure   _____
5. cabin   _____
6. interesting   _____
7. settler   _____
8. automobile   _____
9. material   _____
10. entertainment   _____

Taking a Test

● Read each phrase. Fill in the oval next to the best meaning for the word in dark print.

1. was **born** today
   - (A) brought into life
   - (B) seen quickly
   - (C) left alone

2. through time and **space**
   - (A) unlimited area
   - (B) mirrors
   - (C) stars

3. watched **television**
   - (A) the game between two schools
   - (B) bad vision
   - (C) picture sent by electric waves

4. a wild **territory**
   - (A) large stretch of land
   - (B) dry land without plants
   - (C) animal living in swamps

5. built a **cabin**
   - (A) small boat
   - (B) new shop
   - (C) small house

6. crossed the **prairie**
   - (A) desert land
   - (B) level, grassy land
   - (C) mountainous area

7. was a **settler**
   - (A) person who writes books
   - (B) someone who takes pictures
   - (C) one who lives in a new country

8. an **interesting** class
   - (A) exciting
   - (B) long and tiring
   - (C) hard

9. stretched his **mind**
   - (A) power to know
   - (B) arm muscles
   - (C) rubber band

10. in the **past**
   - (A) time to come
   - (B) here and now
   - (C) time gone by

Challenging Yourself: Scrambled Words

● The letters in each of your vocabulary words have been scrambled. Use the word list to help you spell each word correctly. Write the words on the lines.

		WORD LIST
1. r o t r y e t i r	_____	mind
2. s l e t r e s t	_____	past
3. r o b n	_____	prairie
4. s p a t	_____	television
5. e i r i a r p	_____	territory
6. d i m n	_____	cabin
7. p e c a s	_____	interesting
8. v i n e o s l i e t	_____	born
9. b a i n c	_____	settlers
10. g r i n e t e s t i n	_____	space

36

Using Words You Know: Report Writing

● Who was Daniel Boone? Look up Daniel Boone in the encyclopedia or another book. Find some information about this famous explorer of unknown territories. Write a short report. Remember to use your own words! The following questions will help guide you in writing your report. What things did Boone do well? What territory did Boone explore? What experiences did Boone have with Indians?

   Use at least three words from this vocabulary lesson in your report.

_____

_____

_____

_____

_____

_____

_____

_____

_____

_____

_____

Lesson 8
A Blue Moon

● Read the story below. The new words for you to learn are in dark print. Think of what these words could mean as you read.

A Blue Moon

People sometimes say that a thing happens "once in a blue moon." They mean that it hardly ever happens. How did such a saying ever get started? The saying might have begun because there have been only a few times in **history** that the moon has really looked blue. Over one hundred years ago a **volcano** blew up. **Huge** rocks shot high into the air. Dust rose high into the **atmosphere.** Then the dust blew around the **globe.** The dust made the moon seem blue.

About seventy years later a huge **forest** fire happened in Canada. A great **amount** of smoke went into the atmosphere. People in that **area** saw a blue moon. **Disasters** that make the moon look blue do not happen often. If someone says she only goes fishing "once in a blue moon," do not **expect** to see her out digging for worms.

Getting the Main Idea

● Circle the number of the phrase which best answers the following question:

What is this story mainly about?

1) how people can make the moon look blue

2) why the moon should have been blue

3) what happens when a volcano blows up

4) how an old saying about the moon may have begun

Working with the Alphabet

● Add the following vocabulary words from the story to the alphabetical list below.

volcano	globe	expect	forest	history
amount	area	disasters	huge	atmosphere

_____   foot

arch   _____

_____   _____

atlas   hire

_____   _____

dirty   _____

_____   volatile

_____   _____

Matching Words with Meanings

● Reread the story. Use context clues or the glossary to match each vocabulary word below with its meaning. Write the letter of the meaning on the line next to the word.

_____ 1. history

_____ 2. huge

_____ 3. volcano

_____ 4. atmosphere

_____ 5. globe

_____ 6. forest

_____ 7. amount

_____ 8. area

_____ 9. disaster

_____ 10. expect

a. very large; immense

b. all the air around the earth

c. to think that something will happen or come; look forward to

d. the record of everything that has happened in the past

e. the earth

f. a numerical quantity

g. an opening in the earth's surface through which molten rock from inside the earth is thrown up

h. a happening that causes much damage or suffering, as a flood or earthquake; catastrophe

i. a part of the earth's surface; region

j. many trees growing closely together over a large piece of land; large woods

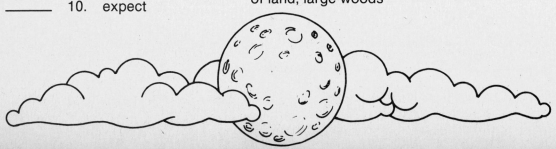

Completing the Sentences

● Read the sentences below. Write the vocabulary words that best complete the sentences.

atmosphere	forest	globe	expected	huge
disaster	history	volcano	area	amount

1. An elephant is certainly a _____ animal.

2. It can pull up trees in a _____ and carry them in its trunk.

3. That nearby mountain is really a _____ .

4. People say that it has a _____ of erupting every 200 years.

5. The fire gave off a great _____ of black smoke.

6. A large _____ of the town turned dark.

7. If the earth's _____ were damaged, everything would change.

8. The land would get colder all over the _____ .

9. Mr. Evans _____ more people to have been hurt in the earthquake.

10. Even so, it was a _____ for many families.

Working with Synonyms

▲ **Synonyms** are words with nearly the same meaning. For example, *begin* and *start, pick* and *choose* are synonyms.

● Match the synonyms below. Write each word from the box on the line next to the word that means nearly the same.

WORD	SYNONYM	WORD LIST
1. huge	_____	tale
2. chuckle	_____	automobile
3. bucket	_____	large
4. moisture	_____	giggle
5. story	_____	pail
6. center	_____	middle
7. car	_____	right
8. correct	_____	dampness

Taking a Test

● Read each phrase. Fill in the oval next to the best meaning for the word in dark print.

1. learn from **history**
   Ⓐ old books
   Ⓑ past record
   Ⓒ school teachers

2. a large **area**
   Ⓐ region
   Ⓑ person
   Ⓒ table

3. around the **globe**
   Ⓐ town
   Ⓑ field
   Ⓒ earth

4. a **huge** tree
   Ⓐ rough
   Ⓑ dead
   Ⓒ large

5. saw the **disaster**
   Ⓐ sad happening
   Ⓑ flowering plant
   Ⓒ funny movie

6. in the **forest**
   Ⓐ swamp
   Ⓑ woods
   Ⓒ desert

7. a **volcano** exploded
   Ⓐ opening in the earth
   Ⓑ star
   Ⓒ cave

8. a small **amount**
   Ⓐ cup
   Ⓑ space
   Ⓒ number

9. didn't **expect** it
   Ⓐ try to hear
   Ⓑ stop to think
   Ⓒ look forward to

10. the earth's **atmosphere**
    Ⓐ air
    Ⓑ land
    Ⓒ water

Challenging Yourself: Word Search

● The ten vocabulary words from this lesson appear in the word search below. Some are written across, while others are written up and down. Find each word in the word search and circle it. The vocabulary words are listed in the box to help you.

```
D V E N T A R E A U
E X P E C T O R Y S
D U S T A M O U N T
I S F A S O T V E R
S M O H I S T O R Y
A O R U N P R L E S
S T E G M H O C S P
T H S E R E C A N O
E O T B E R G N E U
R G L O B E L O C A
```

WORD LIST

history

huge

volcano

atmosphere

globe

forest

amount

area

disaster

expect

41

Using Words You Know: Creative Writing

● "Once in a blue moon" is an expression. Expressions are everyday sayings. It is not always known how these expressions started. Read the expressions below. Choose one that you like and write a funny story telling how that expression might have begun. The following questions will help guide you in writing your story. Where does your story take place? What happens? Who first says the expression? Then draw a picture to go with your story.

- It's raining cats and dogs.
- He raced the clock.
- Button your lip!
- You're in the dog house.
- Go jump in the lake!

Use at least three vocabulary words from this lesson in your story.

Lesson 9
Lucille Ball

● Read the story below. The new words for you to learn are in dark print. Think of what these words could mean as you read.

Lucille Ball

Lucille Ball is one of the best-known television stars ever. Many of your parents were not even born when her TV shows started. Her first **series,** "I Love Lucy," began in the **autumn** of 1951. In six months it was **ranked** number one. The show was very good. It won more than 200 **awards.** Lucy starred in two later series. All of her shows have been shown again and again in **reruns** over the years. They are still shown on daytime television. The shows are shown around the world. The speech has been changed to other **languages.**

One man **figured** out an interesting **fact.** He said that more people have seen Lucy more often than any other **human** who ever lived. Lucy's shows are ranked among the greatest television hits of all time. Just think. When you watch a Lucy show, you laugh at jokes that have tickled the world for half a **lifetime.**

Getting the Main Idea

● Circle the number of the phrase which best answers the following question:

What is this story mainly about?

1) daytime television

2) funny jokes

3) a television star who is enjoyed by many

4) why people laugh at jokes

Working with the Alphabet

● Add the following vocabulary words from the story to the alphabetical list below.

languages   reruns   series   figured   human

autumn   awards   fact   lifetime   ranked

auction

_____

_____

awful

_____

fast

_____

file

_____

_____

law

_____

moon

_____

rash

_____

Matching Words with Meanings

● Reread the story. Use context clues or the glossary to match each vocabulary word below with its meaning. Write the letter of the meaning on the line next to the word.

_____ 1. series

_____ 2. autumn

_____ 3. rank

_____ 4. award

_____ 5. language

_____ 6. figure

_____ 7. fact

_____ 8. rerun

_____ 9. human

_____ 10. lifetime

a. something given by the decision of a judge; prize

b. to place in a certain order

c. human speech or writing that stands for speech

d. to find the answer by using arithmetic; calculate

e. the length of time that someone or something lives or lasts

f. a repeat showing of a movie, taped TV program, etc.

g. the season of the year that comes between summer and winter; fall

h. television program seen regularly; a number of things coming one after another

i. a thing that has actually happened or that is really true

j. that is a person or that has to do with people in general

Completing the Sentences

● Read the sentences below. Write the vocabulary words that best complete the sentences.

series   ranked   languages   facts   human

autumn   awards   figured   reruns   lifetime

1. The judges gave _____ to three pupils for their paintings.

2. Greg's father can speak three _____ as well as English.

3. We start school in the _____ and finish in the spring.

4. The actor was to star in his sixth _____ on television.

5. Mrs. Tate _____ out the arithmetic problem on the chalkboard.

6. My dad likes to watch _____ of old TV programs.

7. I have learned all of the addition and multiplication _____.

8. It was a once-in-a- _____ opportunity!

9. That doll is so large it looked just like a real _____ being.

10. Our football team is _____ in first place!

Working with Compound Words

▲ A **compound word** is a word made up of two smaller words. For example, *football* and *cupcake* are compound words.

● Read each meaning below. Underline the two words in the meaning that form a compound word. Then write the compound word on the line.

MEANING	COMPOUND WORD
1. the time of a life	_____
2. a house for a dog	_____
3. a fish shaped like a star	_____
4. a coat to wear in rain	_____
5. a brush used to paint	_____
6. corn that will pop	_____
7. a flake of snow	_____
8. the day of your birth	_____
9. a bird that is blue	_____
10. a burn from the sun	_____

Taking a Test

● Read each phrase. Fill in the oval next to the best meaning for the word in dark print.

1. in the **autumn**
   Ⓐ spring
   Ⓑ summer
   Ⓒ fall

2. knows the **language**
   Ⓐ speech of a people
   Ⓑ number of words
   Ⓒ spelling

3. a **human** bone
   Ⓐ from a fish
   Ⓑ of a person
   Ⓒ broken

4. watch **reruns** on TV
   Ⓐ new programs
   Ⓑ funny programs
   Ⓒ repeat programs

5. in a new **series**
   Ⓐ hurry
   Ⓑ TV program
   Ⓒ trouble

6. **ranked** in first place
   Ⓐ placed in order
   Ⓑ found
   Ⓒ won

7. **figure** the answer
   Ⓐ write
   Ⓑ find
   Ⓒ tell

8. gave the **award**
   Ⓐ prize
   Ⓑ speech
   Ⓒ paper

9. told the **facts**
   Ⓐ made-up stories
   Ⓑ true happenings
   Ⓒ right directions

10. lasted a **lifetime**
    Ⓐ short while
    Ⓑ an hour
    Ⓒ time something lives

Challenging Yourself: Analogies

▲ **Analogies** show us the relationships between things. For example, *train* is to *track* as *car* is to *road*. *Nose* is to *smell* as *eye* is to *sight*.

● Complete the following analogies using the words listed in the box below.

WORD LIST		
lifetime	month	fact
autumn	human	bushel

1. **day** is to **week** as _____ is to **year**

2. _____ is to **leaves** as **winter** is to **snow**

3. **water** is to **gallon** as **apples** is to _____

4. _____ is to **compound** as **don't** is to **contraction**

5. _____ is to **truth** as **opinion** is to **belief**

6. **person** is to _____ as **animal** is to **beast**

Using Words You Know: Persuasive Writing

● Look at the picture below. What is your favorite television show? Pretend that your best friend likes another program better. Write three sentences trying to get your friend to watch your favorite show. The following questions will help guide you in writing your sentences. What is the show about? Who stars in the show? Why do you think the show is so good?

   Use at least three words from this vocabulary lesson in your sentences.

_____

_____

_____

_____

_____

_____

_____

_____

_____

_____

Lesson 10
A Mystery House

● Read the story below. The new words for you to learn are in dark print. Think of what these words could mean as you read.

A Mystery House

Sara Winchester's house is a big **mystery.** It has stairs that go nowhere. Doors open into **blank** walls. Some rooms are only a few inches across.

How did Sara's house get to be so **crazy?** It seems that Sara believed that she would have good **fortune** as long as she was building her house. Sara never wanted her luck to run out. She never stopped building it. She bought a **regular** house. Then she kept **carpenters** busy adding to it. They worked day and night for years. They built room after room. They made secret **passages** and long stairways with tiny, tiny steps. As Sara gave them new **orders** for building, she did not **plan** well. That is why Sara's house is so strange.

By the time Sara died in 1922 at the age of 82, her house was huge. It had more than 150 rooms and was eight stories high. The place even had **elevators.** Today many people stop in San José, California, to see Sara's mystery mansion.

Getting the Main Idea

● Circle the number of the title which best answers the following question:

Which of these names would best fit this story?

1) "The Life of Sara Winchester"

2) "A Funny House Built by a Strange Lady"

3) "Stairs That Go Nowhere"

4) "The Carpenters Who Built a House"

Working with the Alphabet

● Add the following vocabulary words from the story to the alphabetical list below.

carpenters   elevators   regular   passages   blank

mystery   fortune   orders   plan   crazy

black   must

_____   _____

_____   _____

cast   organ

_____   _____

_____   _____

else   please

_____   _____

Matching Words with Meanings

● Reread the story. Use context clues or the glossary to match each vocabulary word below with its meaning. Write the letter of the meaning on the line next to the word.

_____ 1. mystery

_____ 2. blank

_____ 3. crazy

_____ 4. fortune

_____ 5. carpenter

_____ 6. passage

_____ 7. orders

_____ 8. plan

_____ 9. elevator

_____ 10. regular

a. a way through which to pass; road, opening, hall, etc.

b. anything that remains unexplained or is so secret that it makes people curious

c. a worker who builds and repairs wooden things, especially the wooden parts of buildings, ships, etc.

d. normal; usual

e. good luck; success

f. to think out a way of making or doing something

g. not marked or written on

h. a platform or cage for carrying people and things up and down in a building, mine, etc. It is attached by cables to a machine that moves it.

i. very foolish or mad

j. commands; instructions

Completing the Sentences

● Read the sentences below. Write the vocabulary words that best complete the sentences.

elevator	blank	carpenters	planned	fortune
passage	crazy	ordered	mysterious	regular

1. The _____ ran out of nails in the middle of the project.

2. They _____ more nails from a supplier.

3. The magician performed many _____ illusions.

4. Trying to figure out how he did them drove us _____.

5. The _____ carried us swiftly to the 68th floor of the building.

6. The office we were seeking was at the end of a dark _____.

7. The Girl Scouts _____ a special trip in April.

8. They would not, therefore, meet at their _____ time.

9. The millionaire had amassed his _____ by the age of twenty-five.

10. Every year he would give a _____ check to one charity.

Working with Prefixes

▲ A **prefix** is a word part that can be added to the beginning of a root word. Adding a prefix changes the meaning of the root word.
The prefix **re** means *again*

● Complete each sentence by adding the prefix **re** to the word in ( ). Write the word on the line.

1. You will need to _____ this dress.
    (order)

2. Please help me _____ the paint from this chair.
    (move)

3. Do you think I need to _____ the meal?
    (heat)

4. Jane will _____ the math problem she missed.
    (figure)

5. If you go back inside, remember to _____ the door when you leave.
    (lock)

6. Ben will _____ the money so there will be no mistake.
    (count)

Taking a Test

● Read each phrase. Fill in the oval next to the best meaning for the word in dark print.

1. paid the **carpenter**
   - (A) worker who cleans houses
   - (B) worker who builds with wood
   - (C) worker who repairs cars

2. solved the **mystery**
   - (A) unexplained happening
   - (B) arithmetic problem
   - (C) written riddle

3. had good **fortune**
   - (A) handwriting
   - (B) manners
   - (C) luck

4. **planned** the house
   - (A) started to build
   - (B) thought about
   - (C) bought

5. entered the **elevator**
   - (A) platform for carrying
   - (B) construction site
   - (C) school zone

6. found a **passage**
   - (A) key
   - (B) hall
   - (C) door

7. a **blank** screen
   - (A) colorful
   - (B) new
   - (C) unmarked; empty

8. **regular** order of fries
   - (A) unusual
   - (B) usual; normal
   - (C) cooked

9. gave us **orders**
   - (A) commands
   - (B) prizes
   - (C) lessons

10. a **crazy** idea
   - (A) great
   - (B) smart
   - (C) foolish

Challenging Yourself: Categories

▲ Words can be grouped to show how they go together. These groups are called **categories.** For example, *tables, chairs,* and *beds* go together under the category *furniture.*

● Read each category and circle the three words that can be grouped together.

1. places with **elevators**

   stores   planes   banks   offices

2. things setting a spooky mood in a **mystery** movie

   fog   thunder   sunshine   night

3. things you **plan**

   vacations   buildings   meetings   sleeping

4. kinds of **orders**

   Stand up!   Here it is!   Turn left!   Be quiet!

5. types of **passages**

   roads   halls   openings   walls

Using Words You Know: Comparative Writing

● Look at the pictures below. Write three sentences comparing the two houses. The following questions will help guide you in writing your sentences. How are the houses the same? How are they different? Where would you rather live? Why?

Use at least three words from this vocabulary lesson in your sentences.

_____

_____

_____

_____

_____

_____

_____

_____

_____

_____

_____

Lesson 11
The Skyscraper

● Read the story below. The new words for you to learn are in dark print. Think of what these words could mean as you read.

The Skyscraper

The first **skyscraper** in the world was built about one hundred years ago in Chicago. The **cost** of land in the city was high. To keep prices lower, builders made buildings higher.

A new way of making the **frame** of a building made tall buildings possible. Skyscrapers are built with **steel** frames. Later the walls and floors are built on the frames. Since the building is built in this **manner,** all of the upper floors can be completed before the first floor is done.

In the last one hundred years, handsome skyscrapers have been built all over the world. The first skyscraper was only ten stories tall. Now the world's tallest building is the Sears Tower in Chicago. It has 110 stories.

Skyscrapers are exciting. Riding their fast elevators makes your **stomach** feel like it has turned a **flip.** Looking over the city from the top of one makes big trucks and large homes look like **models.**

People from **jungle** tribes think skyscrapers are strange. "How long," one asked, "did it take to **carve** this out of the mountain?"

Getting the Sequence

● Circle the number of the sentence which best answers the following question:

Which of these came first in the story?

1) The Sears Tower was built in Chicago.

2) Skyscrapers were built around the world.

3) The first ten-story building was built in Chicago.

4) A person from the jungle asked a question about skyscrapers.

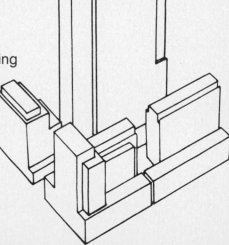

Working with the Alphabet

● Add the following vocabulary words from the story to the alphabetical list below.

stomach   carve   skyscraper   manner   flip

frame   jungle   steel   cost   models

captain   malt

_____   _____

_____   _____

cough   skip

_____   _____

_____   _____

freedom   stir

_____   _____

Matching Words with Meanings

● Reread the story. Use context clues or the glossary to match each vocabulary word below with its meaning. Write the letter of the meaning on the line next to the word.

_____ 1. skyscraper   a. land thickly covered with trees, vines, etc., as in the tropics

_____ 2. cost   b. to make by cutting or as if by cutting

_____ 3. frame   c. the large, hollow organ into which food goes after it is swallowed

_____ 4. steel   d. a hard, tough metal made of iron mixed with a little carbon

_____ 5. manner   e. amount of money, time, work, etc. asked or paid for something; price

_____ 6. stomach   f. a very tall building

_____ 7. flip   g. the support or skeleton around which a thing is built and that gives the thing its shape; framework

_____ 8. model   h. a small copy of something

_____ 9. jungle   i. to turn over quickly

_____ 10. carve   j. a way in which something happens or is done; style

Completing the Sentences

● Read the sentences below. Write the vocabulary words that best complete the sentences.

jungle	flips	cost	skyscraper	manner
stomach	steel	models	carving	frame

1. Mother bought me a new book about animals that live in the _____ .

2. She said it _____ more than any other book because it has so many colored pictures.

3. We traveled to the top of the _____ in a fast elevator.

4. My _____ felt funny when we reached the top!

5. One of John's hobbies is _____ animals from bars of soap.

6. His other hobby is making and collecting _____ of airplanes.

7. Sherry can turn _____ better than any other student in our gym class.

8. The _____ in which she does back bends makes them seem easy.

9. David watched as the men put up the _____ for the door.

10. It was made of _____ , but the door was made of wood.

Working with Homonyms

▲ **Homonyms** are words that sound alike but have different meanings and spellings. For example, *there* and *their* are homonyms.
● Draw lines to match the homonyms below.

1. herd   a. sale

2. plain   b. meat

3. sail   c. plane

4. meet   d. heard

● Use the homonyms from above to complete the sentences below.

a. Mary _____ the news on the radio.

b. Dad learned to _____ on Crystal Lake.

c. Joey will _____ Steven in front of the school.

d. The store will have a _____ on clothes this week.

Taking a Test

● Read each phrase. Fill in the oval next to the the best meaning for the word in dark print.

1. built a **skyscraper**
   - Ⓐ very tall building
   - Ⓑ log cabin
   - Ⓒ airport tower

2. **flipped** a coin
   - Ⓐ grabbed quickly
   - Ⓑ found
   - Ⓒ turned over

3. a small **stomach**
   - Ⓐ arm muscle
   - Ⓑ body organ for food
   - Ⓒ blouse with sleeves

4. a hot **jungle**
   - Ⓐ tropical land
   - Ⓑ burner on a stove
   - Ⓒ chocolate drink

5. asked the **cost**
   - Ⓐ clerk
   - Ⓑ price
   - Ⓒ size

6. **carved** a statue
   - Ⓐ cut
   - Ⓑ drew
   - Ⓒ painted

7. bent the **frame**
   - Ⓐ post
   - Ⓑ fence
   - Ⓒ support

8. in a quiet **manner**
   - Ⓐ time
   - Ⓑ street
   - Ⓒ way

9. built a **model**
   - Ⓐ go cart
   - Ⓑ small copy
   - Ⓒ ship

10. made of **steel**
   - Ⓐ hard metal
   - Ⓑ rough wood
   - Ⓒ smooth brick

Challenging Yourself: Picture Identification

● Look at the pictures below. Write the vocabulary word from the word list that is suggested by each picture.

WORD LIST			
stomach	cost	carve	model
frame	skyscraper	jungle	flip

1.

_____

2.

_____

3.

_____

4.

_____

5.

_____

6.

_____

7.

_____

8.

_____

Using Words You Know: Descriptive Writing

● Look at the picture below. Write three sentences telling about the skyscraper. The following questions will help guide you in writing your sentences. How large is the building? What is the building made of? What do you see as you look at the building?

Use at least three words from this vocabulary lesson in your sentences.

_____

_____

_____

_____

_____

_____

_____

_____

_____

_____

Lesson 12
The Black Widow

● Read the story below. The new words for you to learn are in dark print. Think of what these words could mean as you read.

The Black Widow

A black widow spider is black, and she is a **widow.** Her **mate** dies soon after they meet. Sometimes she **dines** on him. She is a **wicked** widow.

A black widow is the only **common** spider that hurts people badly. Her bite can even **cause** people to die.

Where do black widows live? They make webs in dark, dry places. Watch out for them when you go into an **attic** or other dark, dry place.

It is good for people to know a black widow when they see one. A black widow could stand on a penny. Her back part is bigger than the rest of her body. It is round and **shiny.** Some black widows have brightly colored marks on top. Others are almost all black. There is one sure mark of a black widow. She has a red mark under her body. The mark is **shaped** like an **hourglass.** Do not pick up a black, shiny spider to look for this mark. This lady can be a killer.

Getting the Sequence

● Circle the number of the sentence which best answers the following question:

Which of these happens first in the story?

1) The black widow dies.

2) The black widow's mate dies.

3) A black widow stands on a penny.

4) The black widow can live in an attic.

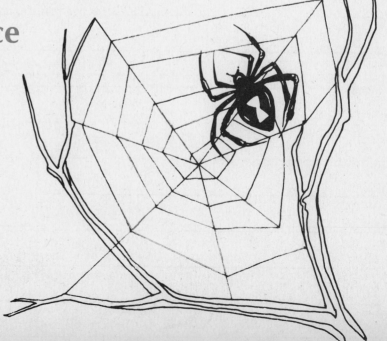

Working with the Alphabet

● Add the following vocabulary words from the story to the alphabetical list below.

common	wicked	mate	hourglass	dines
widow	shiny	attic	cause	shaped

attest   house

_____   _____

cattle   shame

_____   _____

_____   _____

complain   ship

_____   _____

_____   _____

Matching Words with Meanings

● Reread the story. Use context clues or the glossary to match each vocabulary word below with its meaning. Write the letter of the meaning on the line next to the word.

_____ 1. widow

_____ 2. mate

_____ 3. dine

_____ 4. common

_____ 5. cause

_____ 6. attic

_____ 7. shiny

_____ 8. shape

_____ 9. hourglass

_____ 10. wicked

a. room or space just below the roof of a house; garret

b. to give off light or reflect light; be bright

c. to make happen; bring about

d. bad or harmful on purpose; evil

e. of the usual kind; ordinary; not outstanding

f. a device for measuring time by the trickling of sand from one glass bulb through a small opening to another bulb below it. It takes exactly one hour to empty the top bulb.

g. the way something looks because of its outline; outer form; figure

h. to eat dinner

i. a husband or wife

j. a woman whose husband has died and who has not married again

Completing the Sentences

● Read the sentences below. Write the vocabulary words that best complete the sentences.

attic	caused	widow	wicked	hourglass
dining	mate	shaped	shiny	common

1. The _____ has lived by herself since her _____

   died ten years ago.

2. Mary found an old _____ in the _____ of her

   grandmother's house.

3. The _____ witch _____ the princess to sleep

   for fifty years.

4. It is quite _____ to see Mr. and Mrs. Davis _____

   at this restaurant.

5. Kevin found a bright, _____ piece of metal that was _____

   like a heart.

Working with Suffixes

▲ A **suffix** is a word part that can be added to the end of a root word. Adding a suffix changes the meaning of the root word.

                    The suffix **less** means *without.*

● Look at the sentences below. Complete the sentences by adding the suffix **less** to the root word that is in bold print.

1. If air is *without* **shape,** air is _____.

2. If a liquid is *without* **color,** it is a _____ liquid.

3. If a baby is *without* **help,** the baby is _____.

4. If your brother is *without* **fear,** you have a _____ brother.

5. If a bus is *without* **power,** the bus is _____.

6. If a bug bite is *without* **harm,** it is a _____ bite.

7. If your dinner is *without* **flavor,** the dinner is _____.

8. If you cross the street *without* **care,** you are _____.

9. If an ashtray is *without* **smoke,** it is a _____ ashtray.

10. If a stamp is *without* **worth,** it is a _____ stamp.

60

Taking a Test

● Read each phrase. Fill in the oval next to the best meaning for the word in dark print.

1. a **common** mistake
   - (A) terrible
   - (B) careless
   - (C) usual

2. the hot **attic**
   - (A) kitchen stove
   - (B) room under the roof
   - (C) weather forecast

3. with their **mates**
   - (A) husbands or wives
   - (B) school supplies
   - (C) pets

4. **caused** the accident
   - (A) saw
   - (B) brought about
   - (C) ran from

5. an oval **shape**
   - (A) vase
   - (B) form
   - (C) hole

6. come and **dine**
   - (A) see
   - (B) eat
   - (C) sit

7. a **shiny** penny
   - (A) bright
   - (B) new
   - (C) good

8. the **widow's** home
   - (A) man whose wife has died
   - (B) person who is married
   - (C) woman whose husband has died

9. the **wicked** witch
   - (A) old
   - (B) friendly
   - (C) evil

10. a broken **hourglass**
    - (A) window
    - (B) mug
    - (C) timer

Challenging Yourself: Crossword Puzzle

● Read the clues below. Use the vocabulary words from the box to complete the crossword puzzle.

WORD LIST

shiny

mate

widow

dines

shape

hourglass

wicked

cause

common

attic

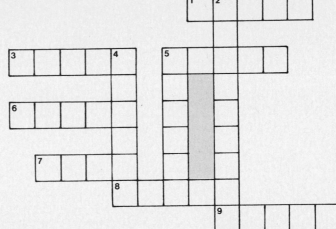

ACROSS
1. outer form
3. woman whose husband has died
5. bring about; make happen
6. space below the roof of a house
7. husband or wife
8. eats dinner
9. give off light; be bright

DOWN
2. device for measuring time
4. bad on purpose
5. of the usual kind

Using Words You Know: Report Writing

● Look at the picture below. Look up *tarantula* in the encyclopedia or another book to find some information about this large, hairy spider. Write a short report. Remember to use your own words! The following questions will guide you in writing your report. What does the tarantula look like? Where do tarantulas live? What do they eat?

Use at least three words from this vocabulary lesson in your report.

_____

_____

_____

_____

_____

_____

_____

_____

_____

_____

_____

Lesson 13
A Smart Gorilla

● Read the story below. The new words for you to learn are in dark print. Think of what these words could mean as you read.

A Smart Gorilla

Koko is a very smart **gorilla.** She has learned to talk. Gorillas cannot make all the sounds that are **normal** for **speech. Therefore,** her keepers taught her to use sign language. The gorilla gets **messages** across in the same way as the **deaf** and those not able to talk.

After some years Koko the gorilla learned six hundred words. She has even made up her own ways to say things. She called a **pill** a candy bean.

One day she told her keepers she wanted a kitten for her birthday. The keepers got her one. She named the kitten "All Ball" because it had no tail. She **combed,** kissed, **tickled,** and talked to the kitten. When All Ball died, Koko seemed sad for two months. Now Koko has another kitten, and she is happy again.

Koko also likes to play with a doll. It looks like a baby gorilla. She **forms** its hands to make sign language. If Koko has a real baby gorilla, will she teach it how to talk?

Getting the Sequence

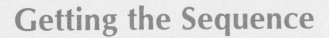

● Circle the number of the sentence which best answers the following question:

Which of these happened first in the story?

1) Koko asked for a present.

2) Koko got another kitten.

3) Koko was sad for a long time.

4) Koko learned to talk.

Working with the Alphabet

● Add the following vocabulary words from the story to the alphabetical list below.

gorilla   speech   messages   pill   tickled

normal   therefore   deaf   combed   forms

color   metal

_____   _____

_____   nose

dear   _____

_____   _____

fort   spell

_____   _____

_____   _____

Matching Words with Meanings

● Reread the story. Use context clues or the glossary to match each
vocabulary word below with its meaning. Write the letter of the meaning on
the line next to the word.

_____ 1. gorilla

_____ 2. normal

_____ 3. speech

_____ 4. deaf

_____ 5. pill

_____ 6. comb

_____ 7. tickle

_____ 8. form

_____ 9. therefore

_____ 10. message

a. to smooth, arrange, or clean with a comb

b. the act or way of speaking

c. not able to hear or not able to hear well

d. to give a certain shape to

e. to touch or stroke lightly, as with a finger or feather, so as to cause twitching, laughter, etc.

f. a little ball or capsule of medicine to be swallowed whole

g. the largest and strongest of the apes, found in African jungles

h. a piece of news, a request, facts, etc. sent from one person to another, either by speaking or writing

i. agreeing with a standard or norm; natural; usual; regular; average

j. for this reason; as a result of; consequently

Completing the Sentences

● Read the sentences below. Write the vocabulary words that best complete the sentences.

gorilla	speech	message	combed	form
deaf	pill	tickled	Therefore	normal

1. My sister is _____ in both ears.

2. _____ , our family is going to learn sign language.

3. My temperature was higher than _____ when I had the flu.

4. I had to take a _____ four times a day for three days.

5. Danny's _____ is hard to understand.

6. A special teacher will help him learn to _____ his words so that his speech is clearer.

7. Mother _____ my hair with a new brush.

8. It _____ my neck and made me laugh.

9. There was an important _____ on the police radio.

10. A _____ from the zoo was on the loose.

Working with Multiple Meanings

▲ Many words have more than one meaning. For example, the word **top** can mean a *toy* or *above.* You need to look for context clues to know which meaning the word has in the sentence.

● Each word entered in the box has two meanings listed. Read the meanings and then follow the directions below.

speech   1. the act of speaking
           2. a talk given in public

row   1. a number of things in a line
           2. to move a boat with oars

● Read each sentence. Use the entries above to find the meaning of each underlined word. Write the number of the meaning on the line next to each sentence.

_____ A. Many Americans listened to the President's <u>speech</u> on the radio.

_____ B. A person who lisps may not have clear <u>speech</u>.

_____ C. Ben sits in the second <u>row</u> from the back.

_____ D. Sarah will <u>row</u> the boat for awhile.

Taking a Test

● Read each phrase. Fill in the oval next to the best meaning for the word in dark print.

1. took a **pill**
   Ⓐ glass of water
   Ⓑ bit of food
   Ⓒ ball of medicine

2. a **deaf** child
   Ⓐ unable to see
   Ⓑ unable to hear
   Ⓒ unable to walk

3. we will, **therefore**
   Ⓐ consequently
   Ⓑ in a time
   Ⓒ at that place

4. **comb** your hair
   Ⓐ braid
   Ⓑ curl
   Ⓒ smooth

5. sent a **message**
   Ⓐ piece of news
   Ⓑ package
   Ⓒ person

6. **formed** a snowball
   Ⓐ threw
   Ⓑ shaped
   Ⓒ caught

7. a **normal** day
   Ⓐ regular
   Ⓑ long
   Ⓒ unusual

8. had clear **speech**
   Ⓐ style of acting
   Ⓑ part of listening
   Ⓒ way of speaking

9. saw the **gorilla**
   Ⓐ ape
   Ⓑ child
   Ⓒ bird

10. **tickle** the nose
    Ⓐ cause pain
    Ⓑ smell
    Ⓒ touch lightly

Challenging Yourself: Word Search

● The ten vocabulary words from this lesson appear in the word search below. Some are written across, while others are written up and down. Find each word in the word search and circle it. The vocabulary words are listed in the box to help you.

```
M E S S E E C T M H S
N C O M B E D I E O R
A L D E N A F C S G O
R I L F O P L K S A T
H E G O R I L L A R E
F O E R M L S E G C S
O M B M A L A D E G P
S A R S L T D O S R E
M F T H E R E F O R E
T H E R E F A R M A C
L N O R L E F D L L H
```

WORD LIST

therefore

normal

gorilla

deaf

tickled

forms

messages

speech

pill

combed

Using Words You Know: Narrative Writing

● Look at the picture below. Write a short paragraph telling what you and a gorilla might say to each other. The following questions will help guide you in writing your sentences. Does the gorilla like living in his cage? What are his favorite foods? What might the gorilla ask you?

Use at least three words from this vocabulary lesson in your paragraph.

_____

_____

_____

_____

_____

_____

_____

_____

_____

_____

_____

_____

_____

Lesson 14
Iceberg

Read the story below. The new words for you to learn are in dark print. Think of what these words could mean as you read.

Iceberg

Icebergs are very large pieces of ice that float in the ocean. The ice is so heavy that most of it is under the water. Only a small piece of it shows above the water. The part above water may not seem very tiny, though. It may stick out of the water as high as a fifteen-story building! Some icebergs have been fifty miles long.

Although it may sound strange, icebergs are formed in the warmest parts of the year. **Thick** ice is **frozen** on land in winter. In warm weather, it begins to **melt** and slide toward the sea. When the ice breaks and crashes into the sea, an iceberg is formed.

In bad **weather**, icebergs cause shipwrecks. Ships are sometimes **damaged** when they ram into an iceberg. A famous **wreck** happened a long time ago. A great, new ship, the Titanic, sank when it hit an iceberg. The sailors had **received** some **warnings**, but they did nothing. Over one thousand five hundred people lost their lives by ramming into an iceberg!

Getting the Sequence

● Circle the number of the sentence which best answers the following question:

When an iceberg forms, which of these happens first?

1) The ice slides toward the sea.

2) The ice starts to melt.

3) The ice falls into the sea.

4) Thick ice is frozen.

Working with the Alphabet

● Add the following vocabulary words from the story to the alphabetical list below.

icebergs	thick	melt	wreck	damaged
although	frozen	weather	warnings	received

aloud

_____

member

_____

_____

recipe

dance

_____

_____

thin

icicle

_____

_____

_____

Matching Words with Meanings

● Reread the story. Use context clues or the glossary to match each vocabulary word below with its meaning. Write the letter of the meaning on the line next to the word.

_____ 1. iceberg

_____ 2. although

_____ 3. thick

_____ 4. frozen

_____ 5. melt

_____ 6. weather

_____ 7. wreck

_____ 8. warning

_____ 9. damage

_____ 10. receive

a. to take or get what has been given or sent to one

b. in spite of the fact that; even if; though

c. the remains of something that has been destroyed or badly damaged

d. the hurting or breaking of a thing so as to make it of less value

e. great in width or depth from side to side; not thin

f. something that tells of danger; advice to be careful

g. a mass of ice broken off from a glacier and floating in the sea

h. to change from a solid to a liquid, as by heat

i. the conditions outside at any particular time with regard to temperature, sunshine, rainfall, etc.

j. turned into or covered with ice

Completing the Sentences

● Read the sentences below. Write the vocabulary words that best complete the sentences.

icebergs	thick	melted	wrecks	damages
frozen	weather	warning	receive	Although

1. We saw many old _____ in the car junk yard.

2. The ice cubes had not fully _____.

3. _____ I was tired, I raced to the finish line.

4. The sun had _____ the snow on the sidewalk.

5. Dad thinks we will have stormy _____ tomorrow.

6. There were small _____ floating near the ship.

7. We heard a winter storm _____ on TV.

8. Mom cut me a _____ slice of cake.

9. Sarah will _____ many gifts for her birthday.

10. Everyone was glad that there were no _____ after the tornado.

Working with Endings

▲ **Endings** can be added to many words. Sometimes the spelling of a word must be changed when an ending is added.

● Read the following rules for adding endings. Then do the exercise below.

Rule 1: If a word ends in a consonant-y, change the y to i before adding **er** or **est.** *funny, funnier, funniest*

Rule 2: If a short-vowel word ends in a single consonant, double the final consonant before adding **er** or **est.** *big, bigger, biggest*

Rule 3: If a word ends in an e, drop the e before adding **er** or **est.** *safe, safer, safest*

● Add the endings **er** and **est** to the words listed. Check the ending rules to see if spelling changes are needed.

	WORD	RULE	ER	EST
1.	easy	1	_____	_____
2.	flat	2	_____	_____
3.	white	3	_____	_____
4.	lazy	1	_____	_____
5.	hot	2	_____	_____
6.	nice	3	_____	_____

Taking a Test

● Read each phrase. Fill in the oval next to the best meaning for each word in dark print.

1. hit an **iceberg**
   - Ⓐ baseball
   - Ⓑ mass of ice
   - Ⓒ pile of snow

2. **although** we want to
   - Ⓐ even if
   - Ⓑ because
   - Ⓒ since

3. change in **weather**
   - Ⓐ where you are
   - Ⓑ conditions outside
   - Ⓒ warm clothing

4. heard the **warnings**
   - Ⓐ cries for help
   - Ⓑ laughter
   - Ⓒ cries of danger

5. a **frozen** pond
   - Ⓐ covered with ice
   - Ⓑ shallow
   - Ⓒ skating

6. the **thick** blanket
   - Ⓐ very small
   - Ⓑ not thin
   - Ⓒ quite long

7. found the **wreck**
   - Ⓐ remains
   - Ⓑ boat
   - Ⓒ treasure

8. will **receive** it soon
   - Ⓐ hear
   - Ⓑ get
   - Ⓒ send

9. it will **melt**
   - Ⓐ change to liquid
   - Ⓑ become a solid
   - Ⓒ move by itself

10. caused the **damage**
   - Ⓐ making like new
   - Ⓑ object to move
   - Ⓒ hurting of a thing

Challenging Yourself: Coded Message

● Finish breaking the coded message below to discover the nickname for the British ship, the Titanic, that sank in 1912. Write the answers to the clues to discover the letter/number code. Then write the letters below to find the answer.

1. even though

   ___ ___ ___ ___ ___ ___ ___ ___
   10 18   3 19 22   1   6 19

2. tells of danger

   ___ ___ ___ ___ ___ ___ ___
   24 10   4 11 13 11   6

3. not thin

   ___ ___ ___ ___ ___
    3 19 13   2 20

4. masses of ice

   ___ ___ ___ ___ ___ ___ ___ ___
   13   2 15 26 15   4   6 14

THE HIDDEN MESSAGE:

___ ___ ___
 3 19 15

___ ___ ___ ___ ___ ___ ___ ___ ___ ___
 1 11 14 13 11 20 10 26 18 15

___ ___ ___ ___ ___ ___ ___
 3 13   3 10 11 13   2

Using Words You Know: Persuasive Writing

● Look at the picture below. The Titanic was found deep in the Atlantic Ocean in 1985. Write a short paragraph telling whether you think people should try to bring up the Titanic or not. The following questions will guide you in writing your paragraph. Would it be worth the cost to bring up the Titanic? What do you think would be found in the old ship? Why would it be dangerous to bring up the Titanic?

   Use at least three vocabulary words from this lesson in your paragraph.

_____

_____

_____

_____

_____

_____

_____

_____

_____

_____

Lesson 15
"Honest Abe"

● Read the story below. The new words for you to learn are in dark print. Think of what these words could mean as you read.

"Honest Abe"

Take a good look at the face on the penny. It is the face of Abraham Lincoln. Long ago he was a great **President**.

When Abraham Lincoln was young, people found that he could be **trusted**. He told the **truth**, and he did not **steal**. Because he was **honest**, he got the nickname "Honest Abe."

Once Abe was working in a little store. He made a **mistake** when he gave a woman change. When Abe found out he was wrong, he **decided** to do the right thing. He walked three miles to give back the six cents to the lady.

Later, Abe **borrowed** money to start a store with a friend. The **business** went bad. They had not paid back what they borrowed. Abe worked many years to pay back all the money. He really was "Honest Abe."

When you look at a one-cent **coin**, think of Abraham Lincoln. He was honest down to the last penny.

Getting the Sequence

● Circle the number of the sentence which best answers the following question:

What happened *just after* Abe found out he had made a mistake?

1) Abe gave a woman six cents.

2) Abe walked three miles.

3) Abe decided to do what was right.

4) Abe made a mistake in giving change.

Working with the Alphabet

▲ In the dictionary, **guide words** at the top of the page show the first and last entries on the page. All other entries on the page are in alphabetical order between those words.

● Below are the guide words from the pages of a dictionary. Use the guide words to decide on which page you would find each vocabulary word. Then write the vocabulary words in alphabetical order under the correct guide words.

president   trusted   truth   steal   mistake

borrowed   business   coin   honest   decided

GUIDE WORDS

born/cold   collect/honor   hop/prevent   prey/try

_____ _____ _____ _____

_____ _____ _____ _____

_____ _____ _____ _____

Matching Words with Meanings

● Reread the story. Use context clues or the glossary to match each vocabulary word below with its meaning. Write the letter of the meaning on the line next to the word.

_____ 1. mistake

_____ 2. honest

_____ 3. steal

_____ 4. business

_____ 5. borrow

_____ 6. coin

_____ 7. president

_____ 8. trusted

_____ 9. decide

_____ 10. truth

a. the highest officer of a company, club, college, etc.

b. that which can be depended upon

c. a piece of metal money having a certain value

d. that does not steal, cheat, or lie; upright or trustworthy

e. to take away secretly and without right something that does not belong to one

f. to choose after some thought; make up one's mind

g. an idea, answer, act, etc. that is wrong; error or blunder

h. to get to use something for awhile by agreeing to return it later

i. what one does for a living; one's work or occupation

j. the quality or fact of being true, honest, sincere, accurate, etc.

Completing the Sentences

● Read the sentences below. Write the vocabulary words that best complete the sentences.

| president | truth | mistake | borrowed | coin |
| trust | steal | decided | business | honest |

1. Beth's dad wanted to start his own _____.

2. He _____ to open a shoe store.

3. Willy _____ a quarter from his sister.

4. He then put the _____ in a candy machine.

5. Kim was elected class _____.

6. She was admired because she always told the _____.

7. Never _____ things from other people.

8. If you take things that are not yours, people will not _____ you.

9. Cheryl told Mrs. James that she had made a _____ in grading her paper.

10. Mrs. James was proud of Cheryl for being so _____.

Working with Prefixes

▲ A **prefix** is a word part that can be added to the beginning of a root word. Adding a prefix changes the meaning of the root word.
The prefix **dis** means *not.*

● Read each meaning below. Add the prefix **dis** to each underlined word. Write the new word on the line.

MEANING	NEW WORD		MEANING	NEW WORD
1. does not <u>trust</u>	_____	3.	is not <u>able</u>	_____
2. does not <u>like</u>	_____	4.	does not <u>continue</u>	_____

● Now choose one of the new words in ( ) to complete the sentences below.

a. The _____ boy used crutches. (distrust, disabled)

b. If you tell lies, people will _____ you. (disobey, distrust)

c. I'm upset because my favorite TV show was _____.(discontinued, disagree)

d. My dad _____ mowing the grass every week. (dislikes, disconnects)

Taking a Test

● Read each phrase. Fill in the oval next to the best meaning for the word in dark print.

1. tell the **truth**
   - Ⓐ a story
   - Ⓑ what is true
   - Ⓒ what you heard

2. **borrow** a pencil
   - Ⓐ use and return
   - Ⓑ pay for
   - Ⓒ take and keep

3. **decided** to go
   - Ⓐ asked
   - Ⓑ began
   - Ⓒ chose

4. made a **mistake**
   - Ⓐ wrong thing
   - Ⓑ rough copy
   - Ⓒ another try

5. a new **business**
   - Ⓐ school building
   - Ⓑ one's work
   - Ⓒ mall

6. **steal** a pencil
   - Ⓐ give away
   - Ⓑ write with
   - Ⓒ take away

7. built up **trust**
   - Ⓐ faith in
   - Ⓑ dislike
   - Ⓒ savings

8. a few **coins**
   - Ⓐ paper money
   - Ⓑ metal money
   - Ⓒ cheap tickets

9. the class **president**
   - Ⓐ leader
   - Ⓑ symbol
   - Ⓒ song

10. an **honest** child
   - Ⓐ sickly
   - Ⓑ careful
   - Ⓒ truthful

Challenging Yourself: Scrambled Words

● The letters in each of your vocabulary words have been scrambled. Use the word list to help you spell each word correctly. Write the words on the lines.

1. d e p r i n t s e _____

2. h u r t t _____

3. d o o r r e w b _____

4. s t h o n e _____

5. k i t s a m e _____

6. s u n i b e s s _____

7. s t r u t e d _____

8. l e a s t _____

9. o i n c _____

10. c d d d e i e _____

WORD LIST
trusted
decided
honest
coin
president
steal
mistake
borrowed
business
truth

Using Words You Know: Narrative Writing

● Look at the picture below. The picture shows George Washington cutting down a cherry tree. There is a story that tells how George was honest about what he had done. Ask your teacher or librarian to tell you the story or read about George Washington and the cherry tree. Then write a short paragraph retelling the story. The following questions will guide you in writing your paragraph. How old was George when he cut down the tree? What did he use to cut down the cherry tree? What did he say when he was asked who cut down the tree?

Use at least three words from this vocabulary lesson in your paragraph.

_____

_____

_____

_____

_____

_____

_____

_____

Lesson 16
A Strange Bird

● Read the story below. The new words for you to learn are in dark print. Think of what these words could mean as you read.

A Strange Bird

A road runner is a strange bird. It lives in the hot, dry parts of North America. This large, **speckled** bird looks like a **skinny** chicken with a long, thin bill and a **narrow** tail.

The road runner hardly ever flies, but it runs fast with the help of its wings. It puts out its wings and takes long steps as it **glides** along **swiftly.** It cannot run as fast as a dog, but it can outrun most people. It can get away from almost anything that chases it. The road runner can dart this way and that. To change **directions** quickly, it just flips out one wing. It can sail across deep **ditches** and glide off **cliffs** to get away.

The bird's strange food makes it helpful to people. It might have spiders and grasshoppers for breakfast. It **gulps** down a **lizard** or mouse for lunch. It may eat a snake for a filling supper. If you ever ride through road runner country, look for this strange but useful bird.

Finding the Cause

● Circle the number of the sentence which best answers the following question:

Why do people think of the road runner as a helpful bird?

1) It makes a good pet.

2) It can dart this way and that.

3) It eats things people do not like.

4) It can run faster than they can.

Working with the Alphabet

▲ In the dictionary, **guide words** at the top of the page show the first and last entries on the page. All other entries on the page are in alphabetical order between those words.

● Below are the guide words from the pages of a dictionary. Use the guide words to decide on which page you would find each vocabulary word. Then write the vocabulary words in alphabetical order under the correct guide words.

speckled	skinny	narrow	glides	swiftly
ditches	cliffs	gulps	lizard	directions

GUIDE WORDS

click/dive	divide/gum	gun/nasty	nation/swim
_____	_____	_____	_____
_____	_____	_____	_____
_____	_____	_____	_____

Matching Words with Meanings

● Reread the story. Use context clues or the glossary to match each vocabulary word below with its meaning. Write the letter of the meaning on the line next to the word.

_____ 1. gulp

_____ 2. lizard

_____ 3. skinny

_____ 4. speckled

_____ 5. direction

_____ 6. cliff

_____ 7. swiftly

_____ 8. ditch

_____ 9. narrow

_____ 10. glide

a. moving in a fast manner; quickly

b. to move along in a smooth and easy way, as in skating

c. a reptile with a long, slender body and tail, a scaly skin, and four legs

d. very thin or lean

e. a long, narrow opening dug in the earth; a trench

f. having small marks or specks

g. a high steep face of rock that goes down sharply with little or no slope

h. small in width; less wide than usual

i. the point toward which something faces or the line along which something moves or lies

j. to swallow in a hurried or a greedy way

Completing the Sentences

● Read the sentences below. Write the vocabulary words that best complete the sentences.

directions	gulp	speckled	narrow	cliff
swiftly	lizard	glide	ditch	skinny

1. The long, _____ snake slithered through the small opening.

2. I saw that it was _____ with many bright colors.

3. A large, greedy _____ ate the fly.

4. It downed the fly in one big _____.

5. The road was so _____ that two cars could hardly fit on it.

6. Often, one car would end up in the _____.

7. An eagle can _____ gracefully on the wind.

8. The eagle can also fly _____ to catch a small animal.

9. We followed the _____ to the mountain cabin.

10. It was located high on a _____.

Working with Synonyms and Antonyms

▲ **Synonyms** are words with nearly the same meaning. **Antonyms** are words that have opposite meanings.
● Look at the synonyms and antonyms listed in the boxes below. Then look at the words in the word list. Find a synonym and an antonym for each word under Word List. Write your answers on the appropriate lines.

SYNONYMS			ANTONYMS		
alike	huge	pretty	slow	ugly	different
swift	rich	healthy	small	sick	poor

WORD LIST	SYNONYMS	ANTONYMS
1. large	_____	_____
2. cute	_____	_____
3. wealthy	_____	_____
4. well	_____	_____
5. same	_____	_____
6. fast	_____	_____

Taking a Test

● Read each phrase. Fill in the oval next to the best meaning for the word in dark print.

1. a **speckled** dog
   - (A) with small marks
   - (B) very dirty
   - (C) having large spots

2. the **narrow** hall
   - (A) very wide
   - (B) small in width
   - (C) quite long

3. **glides** on ice
   - (A) moves with difficulty
   - (B) hardly moves
   - (C) moves easily

4. **skinny** arms
   - (A) long
   - (B) thin
   - (C) fat

5. moves **swiftly**
   - (A) quickly
   - (B) slowly
   - (C) quietly

6. in that **direction**
   - (A) way up the road
   - (B) line along which something lies
   - (C) question about traveling

7. **gulp** the water
   - (A) sip
   - (B) pour out
   - (C) swallow in a hurry

8. along the **cliff**
   - (A) bridge over a river
   - (B) steep face of rock
   - (C) path in the woods

9. in the **ditch**
   - (A) trench
   - (B) cement strip along a road
   - (C) grassy area in a park

10. small **lizard**
   - (A) bug
   - (B) reptile
   - (C) spider

Challenging Yourself: Categories

▲ Words can be grouped to show how they go together. These groups are called **categories.** For example, *spoon, fork,* and *knife* go together under the category *things you use to eat.*
● Read each category and circle the three words that can be grouped together.

1. things that **glide**

   birds   planes   skaters   rabbits

2. parts of a **lizard**

   fins   tail   body   head

3. things you **gulp**

   juice   milk   toothpaste   food

4. things that can be **speckled**

   eggs   walls   paintings   spoons

5. things that are **swift**

   rabbit   turtle   cheetah   horse

Using Words You Know: Comparative Writing

Look at the pictures below. Write three sentences comparing the road runner and the parrot. The following questions will help guide you in writing your sentences. What do you see covering each bird? How large is each bird? How are the birds different?

Use at least three words from this vocabulary lesson in your sentences.

_____

_____

_____

_____

_____

_____

_____

_____

_____

_____

_____

Lesson 17
A Beautiful Old Palace

● Read the story below. The new words for you to learn are in dark print. Think of what these words could mean as you read.

A Beautiful Old Palace

Long ago in Granada, Spain, people built a wonderful **palace.** The palace was called Alhambra (ol om'bro), which means a "red house." Over the years parts of Alhambra have been torn down by **wars** or **destroyed** by **earthquakes.** People keep **rebuilding** it. Today people from all over the world want to see it.

Alhambra is big and beautiful. It is so large it would take an hour to walk around it. What makes Alhambra famous is not its size, but its beauty. Some walls were carved to look like stone **lace.** Water danced in the many fountains throughout the **structure.** Quiet pools were like large mirrors. Beautiful plants bloomed on the **patios.** Lovely pictures were painted on the walls.

An old story goes that there are **ghosts** living at Alhambra. It is said that people who once lived there **refused** to go away after they died. Alhambra was just too beautiful to leave!

Finding the Cause

● Circle the number of the sentence which best answers the following question:

Why do people all over the world want to see Alhambra?

1) It was destroyed by the earthquakes.

2) It is beautiful.

3) They are looking for ghosts.

4) It is the largest building in the world.

Working with the Alphabet

▲ In the dictionary, **guide words** at the top of the page show the first and last entries on the page. All other entries on the page are in alphabetical order between those words.

● Below are the guide words from the pages of a dictionary. Use the guide words to decide on which page you would find each vocabulary word. Then write the vocabulary words in alphabetical order under the correct guide words.

| palace | wars | destroyed | earthquakes | lace |
| structure | patios | ghosts | refused | rebuilding |

GUIDE WORDS

desk/east	eat/parade	past/receive	red/warts
_____	_____	_____	_____
_____	_____	_____	_____
_____	_____	_____	_____

Matching Words with Meanings

● Reread the story. Use context clues or the glossary to match each vocabulary word below with its meaning. Write the letter of the meaning on the line next to the word.

_____ 1. patio

_____ 2. refuse

_____ 3. destroy

_____ 4. palace

_____ 5. structure

_____ 6. ghost

_____ 7. lace

_____ 8. rebuild

_____ 9. war

_____ 10. earthquake

a. to put an end to by breaking up, tearing down, ruining, or spoiling

b. something built; a building, bridge, dam, etc.

c. to say that one will not take something that is offered; reject

d. any large, splendid building

e. fighting with weapons between countries or parts of a country

f. a fabric of thread woven into fancy designs with many openings like those in a net

g. a shaking or trembling of the ground, caused by the shifting of underground rock or by the action of a volcano

h. a pale, shadowy form that some people think they can see and that is supposed to be the spirit of a dead person

i. to build again, especially something that was damaged, ruined, etc.

j. a paved area near a house, with chairs, tables, etc. for outdoor lounging, dining, etc.

Completing the Sentences

● Read the sentences below. Write the vocabulary words that best complete the sentences.

palace	refuses	earthquake	structures	war
patio	destroyed	rebuilding	ghost	lace

1. Tina's mother used Grandmother's white _____ tablecloth for the party.

2. We have a picnic table and a grill on our _____.

3. Mrs. Kent saw the royal family's _____ when she visited London.

4. The electric company is _____ the tower that fell during the storm.

5. Acme Construction Company builds large _____ like the Merriman Bridge.

6. My dog _____ to eat anything except canned dog food or table scraps.

7. Several homes were _____ by the fire.

8. These large cracks in the ground were caused by an _____.

9. Dad likes to watch old _____ movies because he was once a soldier.

10. I dressed up like a _____ for the Halloween costume party.

Working with Antonyms

▲ **Antonyms** are words that have opposite meanings.

● Use the word list to find an antonym for each puzzle word shown. Then write the antonyms in the boxes.

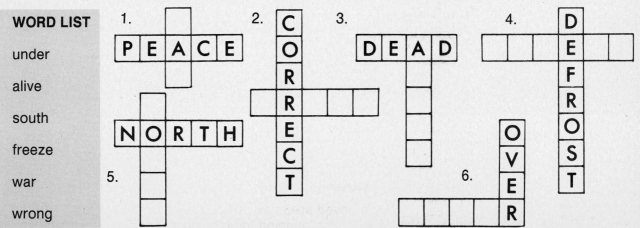

WORD LIST

under

alive

south

freeze

war

wrong

1. P E A C E

2. C O R R E C T

3. D E A D

4. D E F R O S T

5. N O R T H

6. O V E R

Taking a Test

● Read each phrase. Fill in the oval next to the best meaning for the word in dark print.

1. **destroyed** the picture
   - Ⓐ ruined
   - Ⓑ painted
   - Ⓒ repaired

2. used for **war**
   - Ⓐ yelling
   - Ⓑ fighting
   - Ⓒ helping

3. built a **palace**
   - Ⓐ small, cozy home
   - Ⓑ skating rink
   - Ⓒ large, splendid building

4. a **lace** dress
   - Ⓐ plain, blue fabric
   - Ⓑ fancy fabric with holes
   - Ⓒ special fabric for dresses

5. **rebuild** a porch
   - Ⓐ make again
   - Ⓑ put under
   - Ⓒ tear down

6. in an **earthquake**
   - Ⓐ explosion from the ground
   - Ⓑ shaking of the ground
   - Ⓒ storm from the ocean

7. ate on the **patio**
   - Ⓐ grassy area
   - Ⓑ kitchen table
   - Ⓒ paved area near house

8. saw a **ghost**
   - Ⓐ white sheet
   - Ⓑ shadowy form
   - Ⓒ dead animal

9. the largest **structure**
   - Ⓐ something built
   - Ⓑ long fence
   - Ⓒ piece of furniture

10. **refused** the offer
    - Ⓐ agreed
    - Ⓑ rejected
    - Ⓒ asked

Challenging Yourself: Picture Identification

● Look at the pictures below. Write the vocabulary word from the word list that is suggested by each picture.

WORD LIST			
rebuild	destroyed	ghost	lace
war	palace	patio	structure

1.

_____

2.

_____

3.

_____

4.

_____

5.

_____

6.

_____

7. _____

8.

_____

Using Words You Know: Descriptive Writing

● Look at the picture below. Write three or more sentences telling about this beautiful palace called the Taj Mahal. Use a book or an encyclopedia to find out about the Taj Mahal. The following questions will help guide you in writing your sentences. What is built on each side of the palace? What shape is the roof? What do the outside walls look like? Where is it found?

Use at least three words from this vocabulary lesson.

_____

_____

_____

_____

_____

_____

_____

_____

_____

_____

Lesson 18
The Oak Island Treasure

● Read the story below. The new words for you to learn are in dark print. Think of what these words could mean as you read.

The Oak Island Treasure

Long ago people **reported** seeing **pirates** on Oak Island in Canada. Years later, three boys found signs of a buried treasure. As they dug they found good signs. Every ten feet they found a wooden floor. Someone had dug there before! After awhile they had to give up without ever finding the treasure.

Other groups tried to reach the treasure and **failed.** One group found a stone with strange writing on it. A teacher found out what the writing **meant.** It told of a treasure forty feet below the stone. As they tried to dig, water **flooded** the hole. They had to stop digging.

Another group came close. They **drilled** down to see what was deeper under the ground. The drilling showed what could be two oak **chests containing** pieces of **metal.** Before they reached the chests, they were flooded out.

So far, everyone who has almost reached the chests has been turned back by water. Maybe that **ancient** treasure is just waiting for you to find a way to it.

Finding the Cause

● Circle the number of the sentence which best answers the following question:

Why did one group drill deeper into the ground?

1) They wanted to hide a treasure.

2) They wanted to see what they would find if they dug deeper.

3) They wanted to find water.

4) They wanted to get the water out of the hole.

Working with the Alphabet

▲ In the dictionary, **guide words** at the top of the page show the first and last entries on the page. All other entries on the page are in alphabetical order between those words.

● Below are the guide words from the pages of a dictionary. Use the guide words to decide on which page you would find each vocabulary word. Then write the vocabulary words in alphabetical order under the correct guide words.

reported	pirates	containing	failed	meant
chests	metal	flooded	ancient	drilled

GUIDE WORDS

anchor/count   dress/flour   flow/pint   pipe/represent

_____   _____   _____   _____

_____   _____   _____   _____

_____   _____   _____   _____

Matching Words with Meanings

● Reread the story. Use context clues or the glossary to match each vocabulary word below with its meaning. Write the letter of the meaning on the line next to the word.

_____ 1. fail

_____ 2. flood

_____ 3. ancient

_____ 4. report

_____ 5. contain

_____ 6. metal

_____ 7. pirate

_____ 8. drill

_____ 9. mean

_____ 10. chest

a. not to do what one tried to do or what one should have done; not succeed, miss or neglect

b. to have in mind as a purpose; intend

c. a person who attacks and robs ships on the ocean

d. a chemical element that is more or less shiny, can be hammered or stretched, and can conduct heat and electricity

e. to make a hole with a tool with a sharp point

f. to tell about; give an account of

g. to flow, cover, or fill like a flood

h. a heavy box with a lid, for storing or shipping things

i. to have in it; hold; enclose or include

j. of times long past; belonging to the early history of people

Completing the Sentences

● Read the sentences below. Write the vocabulary words that best complete the sentences.

meant	metal	failed	drilled	pirates
reported	ancient	chest	flooded	contains

1. Everyone in our class _____ on a different subject.

2. I wrote a report on _____ who sailed in ships long ago.

3. A deep hole was _____ in our back yard.

4. We _____ to find water for a well.

5. Mrs. Steven was upset because her kitchen was _____ with water.

6. She _____ to turn off the faucet but had forgotten.

7. The museum has many _____ things from foreign countries.

8. One old _____ was covered with different kinds of jewels.

9. My dad has a _____ box on his bureau.

10. It _____ coins from many countries.

Working with Multiple Meanings

▲ Many words have more than one meaning. For example, the word *bat* can mean an *animal* or a *wooden club*. You need to look for context clues to know which meaning the word has in the sentence.

● Each word entered in the box has two or three meanings listed. Read the meanings and then follow the directions below.

drill 1. a tool with a sharp point
      2. to practice over and over
chest 1. a heavy box with a lid
      2. a piece of furniture with drawers
      3. upper part of the body

● Read each sentence. Use the entries above to find the meaning of each underlined word. Write the number of the meaning on the line next to each sentence.

_____ a. I folded my clothes and put them in the <u>chest</u> next to my bed.

_____ b. Dad went to work even though he has a bad <u>chest</u> cold.

_____ c. Mother has a small jewelry <u>chest</u> for her rings and necklaces.

_____ d. Every day our teacher <u>drills</u> us on our multiplication facts.

90 _____ e. The carpenter has an electric <u>drill</u> that he uses to make holes.

Taking a Test

● Read each phrase. Fill in the oval next to the best meaning for the word in dark print.

1. **contains** my flowers
   - Ⓐ has
   - Ⓑ gives
   - Ⓒ receives

2. dressed like a **pirate**
   - Ⓐ person in the navy
   - Ⓑ one who robs ships
   - Ⓒ captain of a ship

3. **failed** to get
   - Ⓐ was unable
   - Ⓑ wanted
   - Ⓒ tried

4. **drilled** in the wood
   - Ⓐ cut a piece
   - Ⓑ made a hole
   - Ⓒ carved a design

5. **meant** to do it
   - Ⓐ had it in mind
   - Ⓑ decided not to
   - Ⓒ did by accident

6. a toy **chest**
   - Ⓐ box
   - Ⓑ drawer
   - Ⓒ closet

7. the **metal** chair
   - Ⓐ element such as iron
   - Ⓑ plastic
   - Ⓒ wooden

8. **flooded** the street
   - Ⓐ ran across
   - Ⓑ overflowed
   - Ⓒ blocked

9. an **ancient** city
   - Ⓐ of times long past
   - Ⓑ new and up to date
   - Ⓒ large

10. **reported** the fire
    - Ⓐ started
    - Ⓑ told about
    - Ⓒ looked at

Challenging Yourself: Hidden Name

● To find the name of the one-legged pirate, write the words on the blanks next to their clues. The answer will appear in the shaded column. Use the word list to help you.

Clue: *Treasure Island* is a book about the adventures of young Jim Hawkins, a one-legged pirate, and their search for a lost treasure.

1. to not do what one tried to do
2. an overflowing of water on land
3. had in mind as a purpose
4. a ruler
5. a prison
6. to tell about
7. a heavy box with a lid
8. of times long past
9. what everyone in the story was looking for
10. a hole in the ground
11. made a hole with a drill
12. at all times; always
13. chemical element that is shiny, such as iron
14. a person who attacks and robs ships

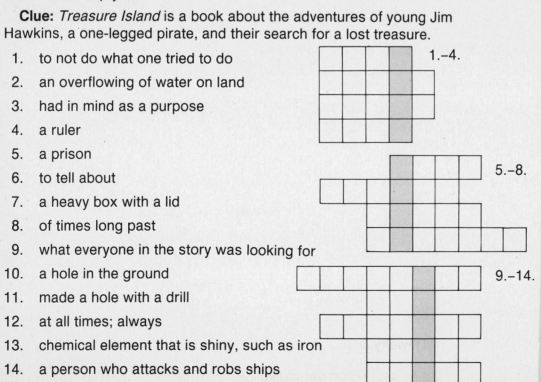

1.–4.

5.–8.

9.–14.

WORD LIST

pit
jail
report
meant
ancient
pirate
metal
king
treasure
ever
drilled
fail
flood
chest

91

Using Words You Know: Creative Writing

● Look at the picture below. Pretend that you are trying to reach the Oak Island treasure. Write a short story telling how you reached the treasure. The following questions will guide you in writing your story. What did you use to reach the treasure? What was the treasure? What will you do with the treasure?

   Use at least three words from this vocabulary lesson in your story.

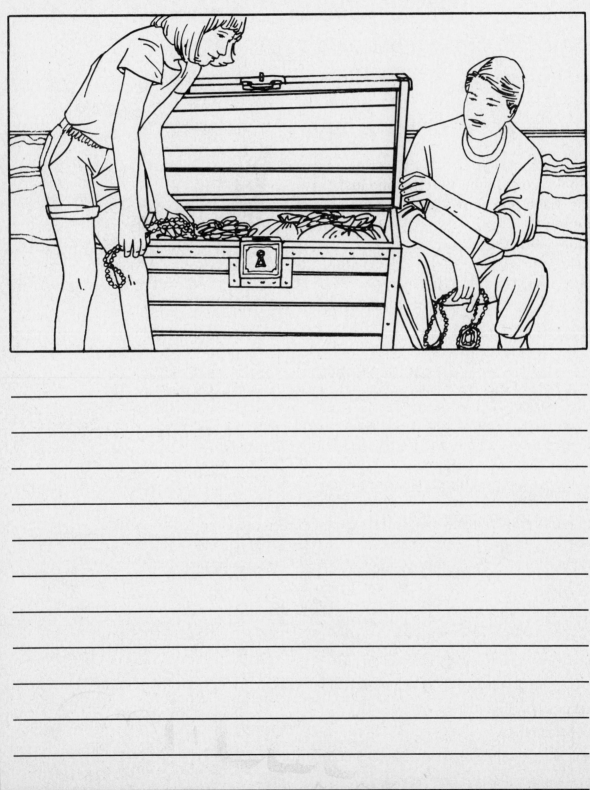

_____

_____

_____

_____

_____

_____

_____

_____

_____

_____

Lesson 19
How Cartoons Are Made

● Read the story below. The new words for you to learn are in dark print. Think of what these words could mean as you read.

How Cartoons Are Made

Do you **understand** how **cartoons** are made? Look at this picture showing a piece of **film**. Each frame has a picture which looks very much like the one just before it. Each one shows just a tiny bit of **movement**.

Cartoonists use this idea to make drawings into movies. First, they draw **scenery** for each part of the story. Then they draw people and animals. They must draw twenty-four pictures for each second of the show. Each picture is only a little different from the one before it. It takes **thousands** of these drawings to make one story. Each picture is colored. Next, the pictures are put on film. A **special camera** is used. These pictures are flashed on a **screen** one after the other. The people and animals seem to be moving.

Real people talk for the drawings. At last the sound is added to the film. Now the drawings seem almost real. As you can see, a great **deal** of work goes into the cartoons that you enjoy watching!

Finding the Cause

● Circle the number of the sentence which best answers the following question:

What happens when pictures with only small changes are shown one after the other?

1) Things seem to talk.

2) Things become real.

3) Things seem to move.

4) People work hard.

Working with the Alphabet

▲ In the dictionary, **guide words** at the top of the page show the first and last entries on the page. All other entries on the page are in alphabetical order between those words.

● Below are the guide words from the pages of a dictionary. Use the guide words to decide on which page you would find each vocabulary word. Then write the vocabulary words in alphabetical order under the correct guide words.

understand	cartoons	film	movement	scenery
thousands	special	camera	screen	deal

GUIDE WORDS

calm/dear	death/mow	much/speed	spend/undo
_____	_____	_____	_____
_____	_____	_____	_____
_____	_____	_____	_____

Matching Words with Meanings

● Reread the story. Use context clues or the glossary to match each vocabulary word below with its meaning. Write the letter of the meaning on the line next to the word.

_____ 1. screen

_____ 2. special

_____ 3. film

_____ 4. scenery

_____ 5. understand

_____ 6. cartoon

_____ 7. deal

_____ 8. thousand

_____ 9. movement

_____ 10. camera

a. a motion picture made of humorous drawings

b. ten times one hundred; the number 1,000

c. to get the meaning of; know what is meant by something or someone

d. a movie

e. a surface on which movies, television pictures, etc. are shown

f. the way a certain area looks; outdoor views

g. the act of moving or a way of moving

h. a closed box for taking pictures

i. not like others; different; distinct

j. an amount; quantity; very much

Completing the Sentences

● Read the sentences below. Write the vocabulary words that best complete the sentences.

cartoons	film	camera	screen	special
movement	scenery	understand	thousands	deal

1. We thought the snake was alive, but it made no _____.

2. Our family enjoyed the _____ as we drove along the ocean.

3. There were _____ of people at the fair this weekend.

4. I did not _____ the question, so Mrs. Davis helped me.

5. Every Saturday morning, I watch _____ on television.

6. Did you remember to buy _____ so we can take more pictures?

7. Grandpa bought a TV with a large _____.

8. This _____ takes clear photographs.

9. Mrs. Thomas likes the small car a great _____ more than the large car.

10. We usually make birthdays _____ by having a party.

Working with Suffixes

▲ A **suffix** is a word part that can be added to the end of a root word. Adding a suffix changes the meaning of the root word.
The suffix **able** means *able to.*

● Complete each sentence by adding the suffix **able** to the word in ( ). Use a dictionary if necessary.

1. She speaks so softly that her words are not _____ .
   (understand)

2. I do not know if this material is _____ or not.
   (wash)

3. This is the most _____ book I have ever read.
   (enjoy)

4. The roads were not _____ during the winter storm.
   (pass)

5. Is the mower still _____ , or does it need repair?
   (use)

6. My answer was not _____ .
   (accept)

Taking a Test

● Read each phrase. Fill in the oval next to the best meaning for the word in dark print.

1. saw the **film**
   - Ⓐ scrapbook
   - Ⓑ page
   - Ⓒ movie

2. a sudden **movement**
   - Ⓐ sound
   - Ⓑ action
   - Ⓒ feeling

3. painted the **scenery**
   - Ⓐ outdoor view
   - Ⓑ colorful walls
   - Ⓒ stage area

4. one **thousand** dollars
   - Ⓐ many hundreds
   - Ⓑ ten times 100
   - Ⓒ number of

5. a small **screen**
   - Ⓐ place for making movies
   - Ⓑ thing for keeping movies
   - Ⓒ surface for showing movies

6. watched **cartoons**
   - Ⓐ children playing in a car
   - Ⓑ movies made of humorous drawings
   - Ⓒ funny stories in a book

7. a **special** gift
   - Ⓐ different
   - Ⓑ wrapped
   - Ⓒ birthday

8. held the **camera**
   - Ⓐ book for keeping pictures
   - Ⓑ box for taking pictures
   - Ⓒ case for a movie

9. tried to **understand**
   - Ⓐ watch the show
   - Ⓑ read the book
   - Ⓒ get the meaning

10. a great **deal**
    - Ⓐ time
    - Ⓑ amount
    - Ⓒ size

Challenging Yourself: Brainstorming

● Read the following **headings.** What comes to your mind as you think about each heading? Quickly make a list below each heading. Don't worry if it is correct or not. Continue on another piece of paper if you run out of room. When you are finished, go back and review what you have written.

things **special** to you

_____

_____

_____

some **cartoon** shows

_____

_____

_____

places where you would want to have a **camera**

_____

_____

_____

things you think are hard to **understand**

_____

_____

what there are **thousands** of

_____

_____

words that show **movements**

_____

_____

Using Words You Know: Narrative Writing

● Think about a day when something funny happened to you. Draw a
cartoon strip and write a paragraph telling what happened. The following
questions will help guide you in writing your paragraph. Where were you?
Who was with you? What happened?

   Use at least three vocabulary words from this lesson in your paragraph.

_____

_____

_____

_____

_____

_____

_____

_____

_____

_____

_____

Beverly Cleary Writes for Children

● Read the story below. The new words for you to learn are in dark print. Think of possible meanings for these words as you read.

Beverly Cleary Writes for Children

Have you met Henry Huggins or Ramona Quimby? Henry and Ramona are sure to make you laugh. You won't meet them playing in your **neighborhood.** You see, Henry and Ramona are **characters** in books written by Beverly Cleary.

Even though Beverly had **difficulty** learning to read, she loved books. Beverly learned to read when she was eight. After that, she read almost every children's book in her town's library. The characters in the books were not **similar** to Beverly. It seemed as though they were always very **wealthy** or very poor. Most of them were from **foreign** lands. Beverly wanted to read **humorous** stories about **ordinary** children like herself.

When Beverly finished college, she became a children's librarian. Soon she began to write the stories she enjoyed telling. Many of her ideas came from **experiences** she had while growing up in a **rural** town in Oregon. She also got ideas from the experiences of people around her. When you read about the adventures of Henry Huggins and Ramona Quimby, you will get to know the young Beverly Cleary and her friends, too!

Finding the Cause

● Circle the number of the sentence which best answers the following question:

Why did Beverly Cleary create her own characters?

1) She wanted children to be able to read about ordinary children like herself.

2) She wanted to be a librarian.

3) She wanted to be very wealthy.

4) She wanted to read about her own life as a writer.

Working with the Alphabet

▲ In the dictionary, **guide words** at the top of the page show the first and last entries on the page. All other entries on the page are in alphabetical order between those words.

● Below are the guide words from pages of a dictionary. Use the guide words to decide on which page you would find each vocabulary word. Write the vocabulary words in alphabetical order under the correct guide words.

ordinary	neighborhood	difficulty	humorous	experiences
foreign	wealthy	rural	characters	similar

GUIDE WORDS

champion/explode	express/hump	hurry/rust	shock/weather
_____	_____	_____	_____
_____	_____	_____	_____
_____	_____	_____	_____

Matching Words with Meanings

● Reread the paragraphs. Use context clues or the glossary to match each word with its meaning. Write the letter of the meaning on the line next to the word.

_____ 1. difficulty

_____ 2. similar

_____ 3. foreign

_____ 4. wealthy

_____ 5. character

_____ 6. ordinary

_____ 7. experience

_____ 8. humorous

_____ 9. rural

_____ 10. neighborhood

a. usual; regular; normal

b. having to do with the country or with people who live there, as on farms

c. trouble or the cause of the trouble

d. a small part or district of a city, town, etc.

e. almost but not exactly the same; alike

f. a person in a story or a play

g. funny or amusing; comical

h. something that one has done or lived through

i. that is outside one's country, region, etc.

j. having wealth; rich

Completing the Sentences

● Read the paragraph below. Write the vocabulary words that best complete the sentences.

rural	experiences	ordinary	wealthy	difficulty
humorous	foreign	neighborhood	similar	characters

My family lives in a _____ town. There aren't many children in my

_____, so I spend many hours reading. I love reading! Sometimes

I have _____ understanding all the words. There are words that look so

_____ I can't tell them apart. Books about _____

lands are very interesting. If I were _____, I would travel to many

of those faraway countries. I also like to read books with animal _____.

These _____ books usually make me laugh out loud. My favorite book,

however, is about an _____ boy who is my age. I was surprised to read

how he had many of the same _____ at school that I have had.

Working with Syllables

● Words can be divided into smaller word parts or **syllables.** Say each word and listen for the syllables. Write the words below leaving a space between syllables. Use the dictionary if you are not sure where to divide a word.

1. ordinary _____

2. wealthy _____

3. rural _____

4. experience _____

5. foreign _____

6. difficulty _____

7. neighborhood _____

8. humorous _____

9. similar _____

10. character _____

Taking a Test

● Read each phrase. Fill in the oval next to the best meaning for the word in dark print.

1. his **foreign** car
   - Ⓐ fast
   - Ⓑ red
   - Ⓒ imported

2. a **rural** area
   - Ⓐ business
   - Ⓑ farming
   - Ⓒ parking

3. in the **neighborhood**
   - Ⓐ small part of a city
   - Ⓑ playground or a school
   - Ⓒ county

4. several **characters**
   - Ⓐ animals in a zoo
   - Ⓑ people in a story
   - Ⓒ books on a shelf

5. a **wealthy** uncle
   - Ⓐ sick
   - Ⓑ poor
   - Ⓒ rich

6. an **ordinary** day
   - Ⓐ sunny
   - Ⓑ regular
   - Ⓒ beautiful

7. unforgettable **experience**
   - Ⓐ something to eat
   - Ⓑ a place to go
   - Ⓒ something done

8. had **difficulty** walking
   - Ⓐ a long way
   - Ⓑ trouble
   - Ⓒ help

9. a **similar** dress
   - Ⓐ alike
   - Ⓑ different
   - Ⓒ unusual

10. a **humorous** story
    - Ⓐ sad
    - Ⓑ funny
    - Ⓒ short

Challenging Yourself: Analogies

▲ **Analogies** show us the relationships between things.

● Complete the following analogies using the vocabulary words from this lesson listed in the box below.

1. _____ is to **book** as **actor** is to **movie**

2. **poor** is to **needy** as **rich** is to _____

3. **common** is to _____ as **uncommon** is to **strange**

4. _____ is to **city** as **county** is to **state**

5. _____ is to **laugh** as **sad** is to **cry**

6. **farm** is to _____ as **skyscraper** is to **city**

WORD LIST
rural
humorous
neighborhood
ordinary
character
wealthy

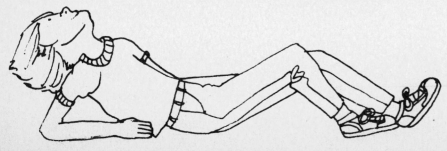

101

Using Words You Know: Report Writing

● Who is your favorite author? Go to the library and find some information about that author. You might look on the book cover or ask the librarian for help. Write a short report about the author. Remember to use your own words! The following questions will help guide you in writing your report. What books has the author written? What is your favorite book by this author and why? Why are these books so popular?

Use at least three words from this vocabulary lesson in your report.

_____

_____

_____

_____

_____

_____

_____

_____

_____

_____

Glossary

Pronunciation Key

a	fat	ī	bite, fire	ou	out	zh	leisure
ā	ape	ō	go	u	up	ŋ	ring
ä	car, lot	ô	law, horn	ur	fur	ə =	a *in* ago
e	ten	oi	oil	ch	chin		e *in* agent
er	care	oo	look	sh	she		i *in* unity
ē	even	o͞o	tool	th	thin		o *in* collect
i	hit	yoo	cure	*th*	then		u *in* focus
ir	here	yo͞o	cute				

Aa

a·dult (ə dult′) **n.** a man or woman who is fully grown up; mature person

al·low (ə lou′) **v.** to let be done; permit; let

al·though (ôl thō′) **conj.** in spite of the fact that; even if; though

a·maz′ing (ə māz′iŋ) **adj.** causing great surprise or wonder

a·mount (ə mount′) **n.** a numerical quantity

an·cient (ān′shənt) **adj.** of times long past; belonging to the early history of people

ar·e·a (er′ē ə) **n.** a part of the earth's surface; region

at·mos·phere (at′məs fir) **n.** all the air around the earth

at·tic (at′ik) **n.** room or space just below the roof of a house; garret

au·to·mo·bile (ôt′ə mə bēl′) **n.** a car; motorcar

au·tumn (ôt′əm) **n.** the season of the year that comes before summer and winter; fall

a·ward (ə wôrd′) **n.** something given by the decision of a judge; prize

Bb

bal·ance (bal′əns) **n.** the ability to keep one's body steady without falling; stability

bat·tle (bat″l) **n.** any fight or struggle; conflict

blank (blaŋk) **adj.** not marked or written on

blind (blīnd) **adj.** not be able to see; having no sight

born (bôrn) **v.** brought into life or being

bor·row (bär′ō) **v.** to get to use something for awhile by agreeing to return it later

busi·ness (biz′nis) **n.** what one does for a living; one's work or occupation

Cc

cab·in (kab′in) **n.** a small house built in a simple, rough way, usually of wood

cam·er·a (kam′ər a) **n.** a closed box for taking pictures

car·pen·ter (kär′pən tər) **n.** a worker who builds and repairs wooden things, especially the wooden parts of buildings, ships, etc.

car·riage (kar′ij) **n.** a vehicle with wheels, usually one drawn by horses, for carrying people

car·ry (kar′ē) **v.** to take from one place to another; transport or conduct

car·toon (kär to͞on′) **n.** a motion picture made of humorous drawings

carve (kärv) **v.** to make by cutting or as if by cutting

cause (kôz) **v.** to make happen; bring about

char·ac·ter (kar′ik tər) **n.** a person in a story or a play

chest (chest) **n.** a heavy box with a lid, for storing or shipping things

cliff (klif) **n.** a high steep face of rock that goes down sharply with little or no slope

coin (koin) **n.** a piece of metal money having a certain value

comb (kōm) **v.** to smooth, arrange, or clean with a comb

com·mon (käm'ən) **adj.** of the usual kind; ordinary; not outstanding

con·tain (kən tān') **v.** to have in it; hold; enclose or include

cost (kôst) **n.** amount of money, time, work, etc. asked or paid for something; price

cou·ple (kup'l) **n.** a man and woman who are married, engaged, or partners, as in a dance

cra·zy (krā'zē) **adj.** very foolish or mad

crowd (kroud) **v.** to come together in a large group

crutch (kruch) **n.** a kind of support

Dd

dam·age (dam'ij) **n.** the hurting or breaking of a thing so as to make it of less value

deaf (def) **adj.** not able to hear or not able to hear well

deal (dēl) **n.** an amount; quantity; very much

de·cide (di sīd') **v.** to choose after some thought; make up one's mind

des·ert (dez'ərt) **n.** a dry sandy region with little or no plant life

de·stroy (di stroi') **v.** to put an end to by breaking up, tearing down, ruining or spoiling

dif·fi·cul·ty (dif'i kul'tē) **n.** trouble or cause of the trouble

dine (dīn) **v.** to eat dinner

di·rec·tion (də rek'shən) **n.** the point toward which something faces or the line along which something moves or lies

dis·as·ter (di zas'tər) **n.** a happening that causes much damage or suffering, as a flood or earthquake; catastrophe

ditch (dich) **n.** a long narrow opening dug in the earth; a trench

drift (drift) **v.** to be carried along by a current of water or air

drill (dril) **v.** to make a hole with a sharp tool

dur·ing (door'ing) **prep.** through the whole time of; all through

Ee

earth·quake (urth'kwāk) **n.** a shaking or trembling of the ground, caused by the shifting of underground rock or by the action of a volcano

el·e·va·tor (el'ə vāt'ər) **n.** a platform or cage for carrying people and things up and down in a building, mine, etc. It is attached by cables to a machine that moves it.

en·ter (en'tər) **v.** to come or go in or into

ex·pect (ik spekt') **v.** to think that something will happen or come; look forward to

ex·pe·ri·ence (ik spir'ē əns) **n.** something that one has done or lived through

Ff

fact (fakt) **n.** a thing that has actually happened or that is really true

fail (fāl) **v.** not to do what one tried to do or what one should have done; not succeed; miss or neglect

fe·male (fe'māl) **adj.** of or for women or girls

fig·ure (fig'yər) **v.** to find the answer by using arithmetic; calculate

film (film) **n.** a movie

flip (flip) **v.** to turn over quickly

flood (flud) **v.** to flow, cover, or fill like a flood

fluff·y (fluf'ē) **adj.** soft and light like fluff

force (fôrs) **v.** to make or do something by using strength or power of some kind

for·eign (fôr'in) **adj.** that is outside one's country, region, etc.

for·est (fôr′ist) **n.** many trees growing closely together over a large piece of land; large woods

form (fôrm) **v.** to give a certain shape to

for·tune (fôr′chen) **n.** good luck; success

for·ward (fôr′wərd) **adv.** to the front; ahead

frame (frām) **n.** the support or skeleton around which a thing is built and that gives the thing its shape; framework

fro·zen (frōz′'n) **adj.** turned into or covered with ice

Gg

ghost (gōst) **n.** a pale, shadowy form that some people think they can see and that is supposed to be the spirit of a dead person

glide (glīd) **v.** to move along in a smooth and easy way, as in skating

globe (glōb) **n.** the earth

go·ril·la (gə ril′ə) **n.** the largest and strongest of the apes, found in African jungles

greed·y (grēd′ē) **adj.** wanting or taking all that one can get with no thought of what others need; selfish

grouch·y (grouch′ē) **adj.** to be in a bad or grumbling mood; cross and complaining

gulp (gulp) **v.** to swallow in a hurried or a greedy way

Hh

hard·ly (härd′lē) **adv.** only just; almost not; scarcely

hatch (hach) **v.** to bring forth young birds, fish, turtles, etc. from eggs

his·to·ry (his′tə rē) **n.** the record of everything that has happened in the past

hon·est (än′əst) **adj.** that does not steal, cheat, or lie; upright or trustworthy

hour·glass (our′glas) **n.** a device for measuring time by the trickling of sand from one glass bulb through a small opening to another bulb below it.

huge (hyōōj) **adj.** very large; immense

hu·man (hyōō′mən) **adj.** that is a person or that has to do with people in general

hu·mor·ous (hyōō′mər əs) **adj.** funny or amusing; comical

Ii

ice·berg (īs′bʉrg) **n.** a mass of ice broken off from a glacier and floating in the sea

in·ter·est·ing (in′trist iṅg) **adj.** stirring up one's interest; exciting attention

Jj

jun·gle (juṅg′g'l) **n.** land thickly covered with trees, vines, etc., as in the tropics ·

Kk

kan·ga·roo (kaṅg gə rōō′) **n.** an animal of Australia with short forelegs and strong, large hind legs, with which it makes long leaps

knot (nät) **n.** a fastening made by tying together parts or pieces of string, rope, etc.

known (nōn) **v.** recognized; noted

Ll

lace (lās) **n.** a fabric of thread woven into fancy designs with many openings like those in a net

lan·guage (laṅg′gwij) **n.** human speech or writing that stands for speech

leap (lēp) **v.** to move oneself suddenly from the ground by using the leg muscles; jump; spring

life·time (līf′tīm) **n.** the length of time that someone or something lives or lasts

liz·ard (liz′ərd) **n.** a reptile with a long, slender body and tail, a scaly skin, and four legs

Mm

male (māl) **adj.** of or for men or boys

man·ner (man′ər) **n.** a way in which something happens or is done; style

man·sion (man′shən) **n.** a large, stately house

mate (māt) **n.** a husband or wife

ma·te·ri·al (mə tir′ē əl) **n.** cloth or other fabric

mean (mēn) **v.** to have in mind as a purpose; intend

melt (melt) **v.** to change from a solid to a liquid, as by heat

mes·sage (mes′ij) **n.** a piece of news, a request, facts, etc. sent from one person to another, either by speaking or writing

met·al (met′l) **n.** a chemical element that is more or less shiny, can be hammered or stretched, and can conduct heat and electricity

midg·et (mij′it) **n.** a very small person

mind (mīnd) **n.** the part of a person that thinks, reasons, feels, decides, etc.; intellect

mis·take (mi stāk′) **n.** an idea, answer, act, etc. that is wrong; error or blunder

mod·el (mäd′l) **n.** a small copy of something

mois·ture (mois′chər) **n.** liquid causing a dampness, as fine drops of water in the air

move·ment (mōōv′mənt) **n.** the act of moving or a way of moving

mys·ter·y (mis′tər ē) **n.** anything that remains unexplained or is so secret that it makes people curious

Nn

nar·row (nar′ō) **adj.** small in width; less wide than usual

neigh·bor·hood (nā′bər hood) **n.** a small part or district of a city, town, etc.

nor·mal (nôr′m′l) **adj.** agreeing with a standard or norm; natural, usual, regular; average

Oo

or·der (ôr′dər) **n.** commands; instructions

or·di·nar·y (ôr′d′ner′ē) **adj.** normal; usual

Pp

pal·ace (pal′is) **n.** any large, splendid building

pas·sage (pas′ij) **n.** a way through which to pass; road, opening, hall, etc.

past (past) **adj.** gone by; ended; over

pa·ti·o (pat′ē ō) **n.** a paved area near a house, with chairs, tables, etc. for outdoor lounging, dining, etc.

per·form (pər fôrm′) **v.** to do something to entertain an audience; act, play music, sing, etc.

per·son (pur′s′n) **n.** a human being; man, woman, or child

pill (pil) **n.** a little ball or capsule of medicine to be swallowed whole

pi·rate (pī′rət) **n.** a person who attacks and robs ships on the ocean

plan (plan) **v.** to think out a way of making or doing something

poke (pōk) **v.** to push or jab, as with a stick, finger, etc.

pos·si·ble (päs′ə b′l) **adj.** that can be

pouch (pouch) **n.** a loose fold of skin, like a pocket, on the belly of certain female animals, as the kangaroo, in which they carry their newborn young

pow·er·ful (pou′ər fəl) **adj.** having much power; strong or influential

prai·rie (prer′ē) **n.** a large area of level, or rolling grassy land without many trees

pre·pare (pri par′) **v.** to make or get ready

pres·i·dent (prez′idənt) **n.** the highest officer of a company, club, college, etc.

Rr

rank (raṅgk) **v.** to place in a certain order

re·al (rē′əl) **adj.** being such or happening so in fact; not imagined; true, actual

re·build (rē bild′) **v.** to build again, especially something that was damaged, ruined, etc.

re·ceive (ri sēv′) **v.** to take or get what has been given or sent to one

re·cent·ly (rē′sənt lē) **adv.** of a time just before now

re·fuse (ri fyo͞oz′) **v.** to say that one will not take something that is offered; reject

reg·u·lar (reg′yə lər) **adj.** normal, usual

re·port (ri pôrt′) **v.** to tell about; give an account of

re·run (rē run′) **n.** a repeat showing of a movie, taped TV program, etc.

rich (rich) **adj.** having wealth; owning much money or property; wealthy

rob·ber (räb′ər) **n.** a person who steals by using force or threats

root (ro͞ot) **n.** the part of a plant that grows in the ground, where it holds the plant in place and takes water and food from the soil

ru·ral (ro͞or′əl) **adj.** having to do with the country or with the people who live there, as on farms

Ss

scarce (skers) **adj.** not common; rarely seen

scen·er·y (sē′nər ē) **n.** the way a certain area looks; outdoor views

screen (skrēn) **n.** a surface on which movies; television pictures, etc. are shown

search (surch) **v.** to try to find

se·ries (sir′ēz) **n.** television program seen regularly

set·tler (set′lər) **n.** a person or thing that settles in a new country

sev·er·al (sev′ər əl) **adj.** more than two but not many; a few

sew (sō) **v.** to fasten with stitches made with needle and thread

shape (shāp) **n.** the way something looks because of its outline; outer form; figure

shin·y (shīn′ē) **adj.** to give off light or reflect light; be bright

sim·i·lar (sim′ə lər) **adj.** almost but not exactly the same; alike

skin·ny (skin′ē) **adj.** very thin or lean

sky·scrap·er (skī′skrā′pər) **n.** a very tall building

sound (sound) **adj.** deep and undisturbed

space (spās) **n.** the area that stretches in all directions, has no limits, and contains all things in the universe

spe·cial (spesh′əl) **adj.** not like others; different; distinct

speck·led (spek′′ld) **adj.** having small marks or specks

speech (spēch) **n.** the act or way of speaking

sprout (sprout) **v.** to begin to grow

steal (stēl) **v.** to take away secretly and without right something that does not belong to one

steel (stēl) **n.** a hard, tough metal made of iron mixed with a little carbon

sting·er (stiṅg′ər) **n.** the part of an insect used to hurt by pricking

stom·ach (stum′ək) **n.** the large, hollow organ into which food goes after it is swallowed

struc·ture (struk′chər) **n.** something built; a building, bridge, dam, etc.

stud·y (stud′ē) **v.** to look at or into carefully; examine or investigate

swift·ly (swift′lē) **adv.** moving in a fast manner; quickly

Tt

tai·lor (tā′lər) **n.** a person who makes or repairs suits, coats, etc.

tale (tāl) **n.** a story, especially about things that are imagined or made up

tel·e·vi·sion (tel′ə vizh′ən) **adj.** of, using, used in, or sent by television

ter·ri·to·ry (ter′ə tôr′ē) **n.** any large stretch of land; region

there·fore (ther′fôr) **adv.** for this reason; as a result of; consequently

thick (thik) **adj.** great in width or depth from side to side; not thin

though (thō) **conj.** in spite of the fact that; although; however

thou·sand (thou′z′nd) **n.** ten times one hundred; the number 1,000

tick·le (tik′′l) **v.** to touch or stroke lightly, as with a finger or feather

trav·el (trav′′l) **v.** to go from one place to another

trust·ed (trust′d) **adj.** that does not steal, cheat, or lie; upright or trustworthy

truth (trooth) **n.** the quality or fact of being true, honest, sincere, accurate, etc.

twig (twig) **n.** a small branch or shoot of a tree or shrub

Uu

un·der·stand (un dər stand′) **v.** to get the meaning of; know what is meant by something or someone

Vv

vol·ca·no (väl kā′nō) **n.** an opening in the earth's surface through which molten rock from inside the earth is thrown up

Ww

wan·der (wän′dər) **v.** to go from place to place in an aimless way; ramble; roam

war (wôr) **n.** fighting with weapons between countries or parts of a country

warn·ing (wôr′ning) **n.** something that tells of danger; advice to be careful

wealth·y (wel′thē) **adj.** having wealth; rich

weath·er (weth′ər) **n.** the conditions outside at any particular time with regard to temperature, sunshine, rainfall, etc.

wed·ding (wed′ing) **n.** marriage or the marriage ceremony

wick·ed (wik′id) **adj.** bad or harmful on purpose; evil

wid·ow (wid′ō) **n.** a woman whose husband has died and has not married again

wreck (rek) **n.** the remains of something that has been destroyed or badly damaged

ANSWER KEY

Lesson 1
Getting the Details
3)

Working with the Alphabet
1. battle   6. greedy
2. carry   7. possible
3. crowd   8. robber
4. enter   9. several
5. force   10. stinger

Matching Words with Meanings
1. d   3. h   5. a   7. c   9. g
2. j   4. e   6. i   8. f   10. b

Completing the Sentences
1. possible   3. forced   5. Several
   stinger   carry   battle
2. robber   4. enter
   greedy   crowd

Working with Antonyms
1. ENTER   4. FAT
2. ROBBERS   5. DANGER
3. ADD   6. TEACH

Taking a Test
1. C   3. A   5. A   7. A   9. A
2. B   4. C   6. A   8. C   10. B

Challenging Yourself:
Scrambled Words
1. stinger   6. robber
2. greedy   7. force
3. crowd   8. battle
4. enter   9. possible
5. several   10. carry

Using Words You Know:
Narrative Writing
Answers will vary.

Lesson 2
Getting the Details
2)

Working with the Alphabet
1. female   6. material
2. fluffy   7. pokes
3. hatched   8. prepares
4. knots   9. sews
5. male   10. tailor

Matching Words with Meanings
1. c   3. i   5. e   7. b   9. h
2. j   4. f   6. g   8. d   10. a

Completing the Sentences
1. sew   6. fluffy
2. material   7. preparing
3. tailor   8. hatch
4. knots   9. male
5. poked   10. female

Working with Homonyms
1. creak—creek   a. or
2. or—oar   b. creek
3. hare—hair   c. hair
4. break—brake   d. heel
5. die—dye   e. die
6. heel—heal   f. break

Taking a Test
1. A   3. B   5. C   7. C   9. B
2. C   4. B   6. B   8. A   10. A

Challenging Yourself:
Word Search

Using Words
You Know:
Descriptive Writing
Answers will vary.

```
I N Y W E K B T M L
T A M O R N F L A U
F T A I L O R F T Y
H R L E A T D P E P
O F E M A L E O R K
E F M S R E P K I A
S P R E P A R E A T
E W S W C B L A L I
O R F L U F F Y O T
S O H A T C H R F Y
```

Lesson 3
Getting the Details
4)

Working with the Alphabet
1. amazing   6. scarce
2. desert   7. search
3. drifts   8. sprout
4. moisture   9. twigs
5. roots   10. wander

Matching Words with Meanings
1. i   3. b   5. d   7. g   9. c
2. j   4. f   6. e   8. a   10. h

Completing the Sentences
1. twigs   6. sprout
2. wandered   7. moisture
3. roots   8. search
4. amazing   9. scarce
5. drifted   10. desert

Working with Endings
1. searches   searched   searching
2. carries   carried   carrying
3. hopes   hoped   hoping
4. drips   dripped   dripping

Taking a Test
1. B   3. B   5. B   7. B   9. B
2. A   4. B   6. A   8. C   10. C

Challenging Yourself:
Analogies
1. desert   4. roots
2. scarce   5. moisture
3. lion   6. search

Using Words You Know:
Comparative Writing
Answers will vary.

Lesson 4
Getting the Details
3)

Working with the Alphabet
1. automobile 6. leap
2. balance   7. pouch
3. crutch   8. powerful
4. forward   9. tale
5. kangaroos   10. travel

Matching Words with Meanings
1. d   3. a   5. b   7. j   9. e
2. i   4. h   6. f   8. c   10. g

Completing the Sentences
1. automobile 6. pouch
2. powerful   7. crutches
3. tale   8. forward
4. traveled   9. balance
5. kangaroo   10. leaped

Working with Suffixes
1. powerful   5. forgetful
2. joyful   6. careful
3. thoughtful 7. helpful
4. colorful   8. cheerful

Taking a Test
1. C   3. A   5. B   7. C   9. A
2. B   4. C   6. A   8. B   10. C

Challenging Yourself:
Picture Identification
1. kangaroo   5. pouch
2. crutch   6. balance
3. leap   7. travel
4. automobile 8. tale

Using Words You Know:
Persuasive Writing
Answers will vary.

Lesson 5
Getting the Details
3)

Working with the Alphabet
1. carriage   6. perform
2. couple   7. person
3. known   8. real
4. mansion   9. rich
5. midget   10. wedding

Matching Words with Meanings
1. f   3. g   5. e   7. b   9. i
2. c   4. a   6. j   8. d   10. h

Completing the Sentences
1. wedding   3. midget   5. couple
   carriage   known   performing
2. rich   4. real
   mansion   person

Working with Prefixes
1. unreal   a. untie
2. untie   b. uneaten
3. unwrap   c. unreal
4. uneaten   d. unwrap

Taking a Test
1. B   3. C   5. C   7. C   9. C
2. A   4. B   6. A   8. A   10. C

Challenging Yourself:
Crossword Puzzle
Across   Down
2. carriage   1. rich
5. couple   3. perform
6. mansion   4. person
7. real   6. midget
10. wedding   8. known

Using Words You Know:
Creative Writing
Answers will vary.

Lesson 6

Getting the Main Idea

1)

Working with the Alphabet

1. adults   6. hardly
2. allowed   7. recently
3. blind   8. sound
4. during   9. studied
5. grouchy   10. though

Matching Words with Meanings

1. d   3. i   5. h   7. j   9. g
2. f   4. a   6. e   8. b   10. c

Completing the Sentences

1. study   5. blind   9. recently
2. though   6. sound   10. during
3. adults   7. hardly
4. allowed   8. grouchy

Working with Suffixes

1. recently   a. Sadly
2. slowly   b. Recently
3. sadly   c. slowly
4. quickly   d. quickly

Taking a Test

1. A   3. C   5. B   7. C   9. A
2. B   4. C   6. A   8. B   10. C

Challenging Yourself:
Riddle

NIGHTMARE

1. SOU Ⓝ D   6. DREA Ⓜ
2. BL Ⓘ ND   7. Ⓐ DULT
3. Ⓖ ROUCHY   8. DU Ⓡ ING
4. T Ⓗ OUGH   9. REC Ⓔ NTLY
5. S Ⓣ UDY

Using Words You Know:
Narrative Writing

Answers will vary.

Lesson 7

Getting the Main Idea

4)

Working with the Alphabet

1. born   6. prairie
2. cabin   7. settlers
3. interesting   8. space
4. minds   9. television
5. past   10. territories

Matching Words with Meanings

1. d   3. i   5. a   7. b   9. e
2. c   4. j   6. h   8. f   10. g

Completing the Sentences

past   space   interesting
settlers   television   born
cabins   minds
prairie   territory

Working with Syllables

1. tel e vi sion   6. in ter est ing
2. prai rie   7. set tler
3. ter ri to ry   8. au to mo bile
4. ad ven ture   9. ma te ri al
5. cab in   10. en ter tain ment

Taking a Test

1. A   3. C   5. C   7. C   9. A
2. A   4. A   6. B   8. A   10. C

Challenging Yourself:
Scrambled Words

1. territory   6. mind
2. settlers   7. space
3. born   8. television
4. past   9. cabin
5. prairie   10. interesting

Using Words You Know:
Report Writing

Answers will vary.

Lesson 8

Getting the Main Idea   4)

Working with the Alphabet

amount   disasters   history
arch   expect   huge
area   foot   volatile
atlas   forest   volcano
atmosphere   globe
dirty   hire

Matching Words with Meanings

1. d   3. g   5. e   7. f   9. h
2. a   4. b   6. j   8. i   10. c

Completing the Sentences

1. huge   6. area
2. forest   7. atmosphere
3. volcano   8. globe
4. history   9. expected
5. amount   10. disaster

Working with Synonyms

1. large   6. middle
2. giggle   7. automobile
3. pail   8. right
4. dampness
5. tale

Taking a Test

1. B   3. C   5. A   7. A   9. C
2. A   4. C   6. B   8. C   10. A

Challenging Yourself:
Word Search

Using Words You Know:
Creative Writing

Answers will vary.

```
D V E N T A R E
E X P E C T O R
D U S T A M O U
I S F A S O T V
S M O H I S T O
A O R U N P R L
S T E G M H O C
T H S E R E C A
E O T B E R G N
R G L O B E L O
```

Lesson 9

Getting the Main Idea   3)

Working with the Alphabet

auction   figured   moon
autumn   file   ranked
awards   human   rash
awful   languages   reruns
fact   law   series
fast   lifetime

Matching Words with Meanings

1. h   3. b   5. c   7. i   9. j
2. g   4. a   6. d   8. f   10. e

Completing the Sentences

1. awards   6. reruns
2. languages   7. facts
3. autumn   8. lifetime
4. series   9. human
5. figured   10. ranked

Working with Compound Words

1. lifetime   6. popcorn
2. doghouse   7. snowflake
3. starfish   8. birthday
4. raincoat   9. bluebird
5. paintbrush   10. sunburn

Taking a Test

1. C   3. B   5. B   7. B   9. B
2. A   4. C   6. A   8. A   10. C

Challenging Yourself:
Analogies

1. month   4. lifetime
2. autumn   5. fact
3. bushel   6. human

Using Words You Know:
Persuasive Writing

Answers will vary.

Lesson 10

Getting the Main Idea   2)

Working with the Alphabet

black   crazy   must   passages
blank   elevators   mystery   plan
carpenters   else   orders   please
cast   fortune   organ   regular

Matching Words with Meanings

1. b   3. i   5. c   7. j   9. h
2. g   4. e   6. a   8. f   10. d

Completing the Sentences

1. carpenters   6. passage
2. ordered   7. planned
3. mysterious   8. regular
4. crazy   9. fortune
5. elevator   10. blank

Working with Prefixes

1. reorder   4. refigure
2. remove   5. relock
3. reheat   6. recount

Taking a Test

1. B   3. C   5. A   7. C   9. A
2. A   4. B   6. B   8. B   10. C

Challenging Yourself:
Categories

1. stores, banks, offices
2. fog, thunder, night
3. vacations, buildings, meetings
4. Stand up!, Turn left!, Be quiet!
5. roads, halls, openings

Using Words You Know:
Comparative Writing

Answers will vary.

Lesson 11

Getting the Sequence
3)

Working with the Alphabet

captain | malt
carve | **manner**
cost | **models**
cough | skip
flip | **skyscraper**
frame | **steel**
freedom | stir
jungle | **stomach**

Matching Words with Meanings
1. f 3. g 5. j 7. i 9. a
2. e 4. d 6. c 8. h 10. b

Completing the Sentences
1. jungle   6. models
2. cost   7. flips
3. skyscraper   8. manner
4. stomach   9. frame
5. carving   10. steel

Working with Homonyms
1. herd—heard   a. heard
2. plain—plane   b. sail
3. sail— sale   c. meet
4. meet— meat   d. sale

Taking a Test
1. A 3. B 5. B 7. C 9. B
2. C 4. A 6. A 8. C 10. A

Challenging Yourself:
Picture Identification
1. skyscraper 5. carve
2. model   6. cost
3. flip   7. stomach
4. jungle   8. frame

Using Words You Know:
Descriptive Writing
Answers will vary.

Lesson 12

Getting the Sequence   2)
Working with the Alphabet

attest | house
attic | **mate**
cattle | shame
cause | **shaped**
common | **shiny**
complain | ship
dines | **wicked**
hourglass | **widow**

Matching Words with Meanings
1. j 3. h 5. c 7. b 9. f
2. i 4. e 6. a 8. g 10. d

Completing the Sentences
1. widow   3. wicked   5. shiny
   mate   caused   shaped
2. hourglass   4. common
   attic   dining

Working with Suffixes
1. shapeless   6. harmless
2. colorless   7. flavorless
3. helpless   8. careless
4. fearless   9. smokeless
5. powerless   10. worthless

Taking a Test
1. C 3. A 5. B 7. A 9. C
2. B 4. B 6. B 8. C 10. C

Challenging Yourself:
Crossword Puzzle
Across   Down
1. shape   2. hourglass
3. widow   4. wicked
5. cause   5. common
6. attic
7. mate
8. dines
9. shiny

Using Words You Know:
Report Writing
Answers will vary.

Lesson 13

Getting the Sequence   4)
Working with the Alphabet

color | **gorilla** | **speech**
combed | **messages** | spell
deaf | metal | **therefore**
dear | **normal** | **tickled**
forms | nose
fort | **pill**

Matching Words with Meanings
1. g 3. b 5. f 7. e 9. j
2. i 4. c 6. a 8. d 10. h

Completing the Sentences
1. deaf   6. form
2. Therefore   7. combed
3. normal   8. tickled
4. pill   9. message
5. speech   10. gorilla

Working with Multiple Meanings
A. 2   C. 1
B. 1   D. 2

Taking a Test
1. C 3. A 5. A 7. A 9. A
2. B 4. C 6. B 8. C 10. C

Challenging Yourself:
Word Search

Using Words
You Know:
Narrative Writing
Answers will vary.

```
M E S S E E C T M H S
N C O M B E D I E O R
A L D E N A F C S G O
R I L F O P L K S A T
H E G O R I L L A R E
F O E R M L S E G C S
O M B M A L A D E G P
S A R S L T D O S R E
M F T H E R E F O R E
T H E R E F A R M A C
L N O R L E F D L L H
```

Lesson 14

Getting the Sequence   4)
Working with the Alphabet

aloud | member
although | **received**
damaged | recipe
dance | **thick**
frozen | thin
icebergs | **warnings**
icicle | **weather**
melt | **wreck**

Matching Words with Meanings
1. g 3. e 5. h 7. c 9. d
2. b 4. j 6. i 8. f 10. a

Completing the Sentences
1. wrecks   6. icebergs
2. frozen   7. warning
3. Although   8. thick
4. melted   9. receive
5. weather   10. damages

Working with Endings
1. easier   easiest
2. flatter   flattest
3. whiter   whitest
4. lazier   laziest
5. hotter   hottest
6. nicer   nicest

Taking a Test
1. B 3. B 5. A 7. A 9. A
2. A 4. C 6. B 8. B 10. C

Challenging Yourself:
Coded Message
1. ALTHOUGH
2. WARNING
3. THICK
4. ICEBERGS
   THE UNSINKABLE TITANIC

Using Words You Know:
Persuasive Writing
Answers will vary.

Lesson 15

Getting the Sequence   3)
Working with the Alphabet

born/cold | decided | **prey/try**
borrowed | honest | steal
business | **hop/prevent** | trusted
coin | mistake | truth
collect/honor | president

Matching Words with Meanings
1. g 3. e 5. h 7. a 9. f
2. d 4. i 6. c 8. b 10. j

Completing the Sentences
1. business   6. truth
2. decided   7. steal
3. borrowed   8. trust
4. coin   9. mistake
5. president   10. honest

Working with Prefixes
1. distrust   a. disabled
2. dislike   b. distrust
3. disable   c. discontinued
4. discontinue   d. dislikes

Taking a Test
1. B 3. C 5. B 7. A 9. A
2. A 4. A 6. C 8. B 10. C

Challenging Yourself:
Scrambled Words
1. president 4. honest   7. trusted 10. decided
2. truth   5. mistake   8. steal
3. borrowed   6. business 9. coin

Using Words You Know:
Narrative Writing
Answers will vary.

Lesson 16
Finding the Cause 3)
Working with the Alphabet

click/dive   glides   **nation/swim**
cliffs   gulps   skinny
directions   **gun/nasty** speckled
ditches   lizard   swiftly
divide/gum   narrow

Matching Words with Meanings

1. j   3. d   5. i   7. a   9. h
2. c   4. f   6. g   8. e   10. b

Completing the Sentences

1. skinny   6. ditch
2. speckled   7. glide
3. lizard   8. swiftly
4. gulp   9. directions
5. narrow   10. cliff

Working with Synonyms and Antonyms

Synonyms   Antonyms
1. huge   small
2. pretty   ugly
3. rich   poor
4. healthy   sick
5. alike   different
6. swift   slow

Taking a Test

1. A   3. C   5. A   7. C   9. A
2. B   4. B   6. B   8. B   10. B

Challenging Yourself:
Categories

1. birds, planes, skaters
2. tail, body, head
3. juice, milk, food
4. eggs, walls, paintings
5. rabbit, cheetah, horse

Using Words You Know:
Comparative Writing

Answers will vary.

Lesson 17
Finding the Cause 2)
Working with the Alphabet

desk/east   lace   **red/warts**
destroyed   palace   refused
earthquakes   **past/receive** structure
eat/parade patios   wars
ghosts   rebuilding

Matching Words with Meanings

1. j   3. a   5. b   7. f   9. e
2. c   4. d   6. h   8. i   10. g

Completing the Sentences

1. lace   5. structures   9. war
2. patio   6. refuses   10. ghost
3. palace   7. destroyed
4. rebuilding 8. earthquake

Working with Antonyms

1. WAR   3. ALIVE   5. SOUTH
2. WRONG   4. FREEZE   6. UNDER

Taking a Test

1. A   3. C   5. A   7. C   9. A
2. B   4. B   6. B   8. B   10. B

Challenging Yourself:
Picture Identification

1. palace   6. war
2. lace   7. structure
3. rebuild 8. destroyed
4. patio
5. ghost

Using Words You Know:
Descriptive Writing

Answers will vary.

Lesson 18
Finding the Cause 2)
Working with the Alphabet

anchor/count **flow/pint**
ancient   meant
chests   metal
containing
dress/flour   **pipe/represent**
drilled   pirates
failed   reported
flooded

Matching Words with Meanings

1. a   3. j   5. i   7. c   9. b
2. g   4. f   6. d   8. e   10. h

Completing the Sentences

1. reported   6. meant
2. pirates   7. ancient
3. drilled   8. chest
4. failed   9. metal
5. flooded   10. contains

Working with Multiple Meanings

a. 2   d. 2
b. 3   e. 1
c. 1

Taking a Test

1. A   3. A   5. A   7. A   9. A
2. B   4. B   6. A   8. B   10. B

Challenging Yourself:
Hidden Name

LONG JOHN SILVER
1. FAI(L)   8. A(N)CIENT
2. FLO(O)D   9. TREA(S)URE
3. MEA(N)T   10. P(I)T
4. KIN(G)   11. DRI(L)LED
5. (J)AIL   12. E(V)ER
6. REP(O)RT   13. M(E)TAL
7. C(H)EST   14. PI(R)ATE

Using Words You Know:
Creative Writing

Answers will vary.

Lesson 19
Finding the Cause 3)
Working with the Alphabet

calm/dear   film   special
camera   movement   **spend/undo**
cartoons   **much/speed** thousands
deal   scenery   understand
death/mow   screen

Matching Words with Meanings

1. e   3. d   5. c   7. j   9. g
2. i   4. f   6. a   8. b   10. h

Completing the Sentences

1. movement   6. film
2. scenery   7. screen
3. thousands 8. camera
4. understand 9. deal
5. cartoons   10. special

Working with Suffixes

1. understandable   4. passable
2. washable   5. useable/usable
3. enjoyable   6. acceptable

Taking a Test

1. C   3. A   5. C   7. A   9. C
2. B   4. B   6. B   8. B   10. B

Challenging Yourself:
Brainstorming

Answers will vary.

Using Words You Know:
Narrative Writing

Answers will vary.

Lesson 20
Finding the Cause 1)
Working with the Alphabet

champion/explode foreign   rural
characters   humorous   **shock/weather**
difficulty   **hurry/rust** similar
experiences   neighborhood wealthy
express/hump   ordinary

Matching Words with Meanings

1. c   3. i   5. f   7. h   9. b
2. e   4. j   6. a   8. g   10. d

Completing the Sentences

rural   wealthy
neighborhood   characters
difficulty   humorous
similar   ordinary
foreign   experiences

Working with Syllables

1. or di nar y   6. dif fi cul ty
2. wealth y   7. neigh bor hood
3. ru ral   8. hu mor ous
4. ex pe ri ence   9. sim i lar
5. for eign   10. char ac ter

Taking a Test

1. C   3. A   5. C   7. C   9. A
2. B   4. B   6. B   8. B   10. B

Challenging Yourself:
Analogies

1. character   4. neighborhood
2. wealthy   5. humorous
3. ordinary   6. rural

Using Words You Know:
Report Writing

Answers will vary.